Oregon's Quiet Waters

Oregon's Quiet Waters

A Guide to Lakes for Canoeists and Other Paddlers

By Cheryl McLean & Clint Brown

JACKSON CREEK PRESS

cover photo of Lost Lake
by Cheryl McLean

Printed in the United States of America
First Printing

Jackson Creek Press
2150 Jackson Creek Drive
Corvallis, Oregon 97330

ISBN 0-943097-01-0

*Dedicated to all of you
who join the effort to preserve
the pristine beauty
of Oregon's quiet lakes.*

Foreword

Oregonians love water. Tell them that 42.5 cubic miles of water descends on their hapless state every year and they'll probably shout hooray. They know that the water will enrich their lives in ways that non-Oregonians don't always understand: through the tranquilizing effect of rain on the roof, through the euphoric feeling brought by watching a creek tumble down a mountainside, through the reverence for nature's power that emerges when you witness roaring river rapids or the thundering ocean surf. But as the authors of *Oregon's Quiet Waters* point out, not all of Oregon's water boldly announces its presence by clatter, roar, and thunder. Much of it speaks softly, like snow floating down onto the Cascade Mountains.

So it is with *Oregon's Quiet Waters*. Here the authors have labored lovingly to find the best of Oregon's 6,500 lakes and reservoirs. They have worked to find the most soothingly quiet of them all, the tiny lakes tucked away in the remote corners of Oregon. Those who enjoy the quiet outdoor life—the almost eerie, brooding silence that pervades so much of Oregon's back country—will be irresistibly drawn to such scenic marvels as Gold Lake, Linton Lake, Charlton Lake, Wahtum Lake, and even the lake with the singularly unromantic name, Dead Horse Lake.

I have visited about half the lakes on their list. Among my favorites are Lost, Clear, and Trillium Lakes, which I have explored in a way perhaps not anticipated by the authors: via makeshift sailboat, using a sail kit for my inflatable raft. Not to worry, though; even the wind is silent in these waters.

—Ken Metzler
Author of *The Best of Oregon*

Acknowledgments

Many individuals participated in making this guidebook a reality. We would like to thank the recreation directors and others of the U.S. Forest Service Regional and District offices who helped assure the accuracy of the lake narratives: Earl Baumgarten, June Cormie, Sandy Gannon, B. Hammer, Sandy Hurlocker, Donald H. Doyle, Bill Stover, Diana Hsieh, Ben Davies, Rochelle Belloir, Chris Jensen, Art Currier, Phyllis Zerr, Jim Galaba, Frank Carson, Bill Otani, Cleon Pitts, Don Palmer, Don Campbell, Phil Raab, and others, as well as Jim Hutchinson of the Oregon Department of Fish and Wildlife and Ted Kolberg of Portland General Electric. Our thanks, too, to Dan Johnson of Portland State University and Edie Ball of the Oregon Department of Tourism for providing photographs.

To those who shared their wisdom and professional expertise in reviewing the manuscript, we give our special thanks: Anne Stainbrook, Ken Metzler, and George Edmonston.

Several important references were consulted frequently while visiting these lakes and in writing the narratives. The first of these is the *Atlas of Oregon Lakes*, published by the Oregon State University Press, written by Daniel M. Johnson, Richard R. Petersen, D. Richard Lycan, James W. Sweet, Mark E. Neuhaus, and Andrew L. Schaedel. The result of an in-depth study completed by these Portland State University scientists, it provides a great deal of specific information about water quality, depth, size, elevation, and much more. The second reference is *Oregon Geographic Names*, first compiled by Lewis A. MacArthur, now in its fifth edition from the Oregon Historical Society. This book served as the source of information regarding lake names. Another very useful book was *The New Henning's Guide to Fishing in Oregon* in its latest edition by Dan Casali and Madelynne Diness, published by Flying Pencil Publications. The guidebook has appeared in several editions in the last 20 years and has served as a valuable guide to fishing in all of Oregon's lakes and streams. Finally, the U.S. Forest Service Publication, "Lakes of the Willamette National Forest," provided a great deal of detailed information on many of the high-Cascade lakes in this region.

We extend our personal appreciation to Lila Swanson for the time she made available during the writing of this book, and to friends new and old who helped us to discover more of Oregon.

—C.M. & C.B.

Preface

Oregon's Quiet Waters is about lifestyle, about the pace of life during those "off" moments, those times when you can relax, be yourself, and take in the peace and tranquility of your surroundings.

Sometimes we like to increase the pace, to capture the certain tension and thrill of whitewater rafting or racing through the windspray on waterskis. But we also need to kick back and quietly savor living in this incredible state.

Oregon's Quiet Waters guides you to lakes where the pace is your own, where you can glide silently across calm waters without being disturbed by the noise and speed of motorboats.

Once you discover these quiet places, you have the urge not to share them, to keep them to yourself so they won't be spoiled. But they're too special not to share, and most of the lakes described in the following pages benefit from protections and regulations that limit the impact humans can have on these fragile environments.

With only a few exceptional exceptions, motors are either prohibited on these lakes or impractical because you have to hike in to them. After lugging ourselves, our backpacks, and our raft on a long uphill trek into a wilderness lake, we decided that certain criteria needed to be established for hike-in lakes. We wanted them to be close enough to the trailhead so that people could walk in with their boats for the day and still have most of the time left for boating or fishing. And for those who planned to stay overnight, we wanted the walk to be short enough that people still had some energy left after carrying all their gear *plus* the extra weight of an inflatable boat. So, all hike-in lakes listed here are less than three miles from the road. Yet despite their proximity to civilization, all rest in wilderness settings, giving you a rich backcountry experience without a back-breaking trek.

Over the last several years, we set about discovering Oregon's quiet lakes. Most of them we found by chasing little blue dots on the national forest maps, knowing little about them beforehand. Along the way we made a number of delightful discoveries, which we share with you here. We also ran into some dead ends and some disappointments, which we will spare you.

We tried to be as comprehensive as possible when it came to motorless lakes to which one could drive, although for various reasons not all have been included. As for hike-ins, we had to be even more selective or consider writing this book in several volumes. If we've missed someplace truly special, we hope you'll write to the publishers so that it can be included in subsequent editions of *Quiet Waters*. Comments intended for the authors can be sent care of Jackson Creek Press, 2150 Jackson Creek Drive, Corvallis, Oregon 97330.

The goal of *Oregon's Quiet Waters* is to give you years of enjoyable discovery. Even if you visit several of these lakes each summer, it will take you more than a decade to explore them all. Happy paddling.

Table of Contents

Oregon's Lakes

More than 6,000 lakes punctuate Oregon's landscape, from Crater Lake, the deepest in the United States, to countless ponds and the like created on farms for watering cattle.

A large proportion of Oregon's lakes lie in the high Cascades, the backbone of Oregon, where hundreds of lake basins have been carved by geologically recent glacial and volcanic activity. Several lakes formed rapidly when lava flows dammed streams, filling the basins with water. Clear and Linton Lakes provide vivid examples of this type of lake. Other lakes formed by volcanic activity fill craters left after powerful explosions. The most obvious example of this type of lake, of course, is Crater Lake in southern Oregon. Smaller and more obscure, North and South Twin Lakes, which lie in the headwaters of the Deschutes River basin, occupy maars, small craters formed by explosions of steam coming into contact with hot volcanic rock beneath the surface. More commonly in the Cascades, glaciers scoured rock basins and formed lakes through the slow migration of monumental ice floes.

According to a recent study by a team of scientists from Portland State University, the water quality in Oregon's lakes runs exceptionally high, as the number of Blue Lakes and Clear Lakes in the state might suggest (21 in all). Water quality suffers most from human impact, whether through improper waste disposal or land use practices or from the waves of a power boat eroding the shoreline.

Even undisturbed, lakes are ephemeral, slowly filling with sediment deposited by tributary streams. Some lakes, such as Sparks and Hosmer, have come a long way in the eutrophication process—a lake's natural process of aging—and the encroaching vegetation will eventually reclaim the land, forming a broad marsh.

Oregon's lakes fill a vital role in the state's water resources. They contribute a wide range of uses, from water supplies for drinking and irrigation to tourist and recreation attractions. The latter function brings to mind the purpose behind *Quiet Waters*.

Quiet Lakes

We've been avid canoeists for many years, both flatwater and whitewater. Maybe we're getting older, or perhaps it's a sense of "I've done that," but in recent years we've found ourselves settling the canoe into pristine, solitary lakes in search of quiet adventure.

After years of paddling around Clear Lake in the Willamette National Forest, we realized that we'd been drawn there not just because of the enchanted clarity of the water or the gorgeous scenery, but because of its sense of quiet, its abiding serenity. The absence of motorized boats leaves a palpable calm. The jangle of oarlocks in the rowboats taps out a slow rhythm, a pace befitting a lake in a mountain forest.

Signs of wildlife

On lakes without motors, you encounter much more of the natural environment. Deer and other wildlife venture nearer when not disturbed by the sound of a motor. And the speed of canoeing or rowing lends itself well to taking in the experience—you simply see more when paddling slowly up the shoreline.

You hear more, too. The first time a beaver slaps its tail in warning you're sure someone just shot a cannonball into the water—it's enough to send you jumping out of the boat.

The shrill call of the osprey signals a time to fish, but just watching these agile creatures gather food provides ready entertainment. You marvel at their vision as they circle high above, then suddenly fold their wings for the swoop and dive, plunging into the lake with a resounding splash and pulling up with their wriggling prey.

At dusk, the electric hum of nighthawks begins as they fly in swift turns after insects for supper. But the real aerialists are the American white pelicans of Upper Klamath Lake. They dance a high-altitude ballet far above the earth's bounds.

On many of Oregon's mountain lakes, the modest little water ouzel busily dips in and out at the lake's edge as if making rounds that must be completed before day's end. A mallard hen leads her parade of ducklings, ever wary of predators.

The lakes of Oregon cloak a fascinating world beneath the surface, as well, readily visible because of the water's clarity. The view below often rivals the mountains and scenery above—what a thrill to watch an otter or a silver-sided Atlantic salmon swim under your boat!

The day wears itself visibly on a lake. At dawn, the glassy quiet of the water's surface reveals a lake just waking. The sound of campers starting their day travels across the water. By midday, a breeze breaks the calm and cools the air, muffling the sounds of boats and paddlers. Then in the evening, the lake seems to settle down again, growing still for the night.

Oregon's quiet lakes offer much in the way of recreation—fishing, hiking, swimming, and, of course, paddling. But one of the most pleasurable activities is simply doing nothing. Just let the magic of the setting and the water clear away all cares and concerns and let yourself ease into the quiet and tranquility of the experience.

The Lake Descriptions

Although more than 40 lakes have been covered in detail, within these descriptions you'll find brief discussions of some 60 more. Most of these lie within the Cascade Mountains, due to their particular geological evolution.

For each lake, the following information is summarized, where appropriate: location, including distance from the nearest major population area; accessibility; size; camping and fishing information; hiking trails; points of interest; other recreation opportunities; other lakes in the area; nearest source of supplies; and specific directions. When planning an outing, use the overall map following this section to find lakes in the general area you wish to visit. An index following the map serves as a key to the primary lakes, and park and recreation symbols indicate what facilities are to be found.

We've tried to cover a broad range of interest and experience, so the lakes included run from large and highly popular Lost Lake to tiny Betty Lake, virtually obscured by its giant neighbor, Waldo Lake. Some lakes offer rustic cabin accommodations and boat rentals; others, the only signs of civilization are the trail and your tent. In some descriptions, you'll find note of nearby resorts or well-developed camping areas so that those less accustomed to wilderness camping can still enjoy the backcountry experience.

Equipment

Canoes, especially, befit the quiet lake experience. The sleek form gently slips over the surface and allows you to glide through bullrushes or against the current of a shallow tributary. Canoes and kayaks maneuver easily, enabling you to travel the length of a lake in a shorter time than, say, a raft or a rowboat. The rowboat, however, carries the nostalgic image of first fishing trips with grandpa, and it provides greater stability in the water and more room for gear and stretching out for a floating nap in the sun. As for inflatable craft, what they lack in aesthetics they more than make up for in portability.

Those exploring the hike-in lakes will want to bring along a number of supplies in addition to the usual backpacking gear. Number one, of course, is a boat, and there are numerous choices. Some hardy souls will portage a full-sized canoe, but for most of us an inflatable is the answer.

When buying an inflatable boat, remember that the number of people it is designed to carry is based on weight, not on the actual amount of space. A two-person boat might bear the weight of two adults, but you may never untwine your legs if two of you paddle it for any length of time. Generally, it's best to subtract one from the number of people the box says the boat will hold, and then expect to be a little cramped besides. If you want the boat to be roomy, subtract two.

For day trips only, weight is not as much a factor as for those packing in overnight equipment as well. Inflatable boats vary greatly in weight, so backpackers are advised to take this into consideration when making a selection. A one-person, four-foot inflatable raft can weigh as little as five pounds, while an inflatable canoe, which is both faster and more maneuverable than a raft, can weigh over 40 pounds. Inflatable kayaks run from just under 20 to over 30 pounds.

Inflatables also come in a variety of shapes and sizes. You can get rafts in one- to 20-person sizes. A good size for a pair of backpackers is the three-person. It weighs around 15 pounds, depending on the brand you purchase, and rolls up to about the size of a rolled-up backpacking tent. Or you can get an inflatable kayak, good for one to two people but not too good for carrying gear by boat to your campsite. They also don't track well on still water, making little S-curves all the way down the lake. The two-person inflatable canoe with directional stakes works better, but you have to decide if the extra weight is worth the additional space and better maneuverability.

In addition to the boat, you need paddles and, unless you're very windy, a pump. Lightweight plastic paddles that collapse into small sections are ideal for backpackers and stillwater paddling, and you can get pumps about the size of a tennis shoe and not too heavy.

Life jackets are a required part of your equipment on the water, and they're generally a good idea. Even on calm water, it's not too difficult to capsize a small boat, and the cold glacier water filling most of these lakes can be a shock to your system, making it difficult to swim. Inflatable vests, which inflate with air cartridges, are available at larger sporting goods stores. However, we found the combination life-fishing vest useful in several ways: it carries your fishing tackle, serves as a life vest, helps you stay warm in cooler weather, makes a nice pillow for sleeping, and is great padding for the backpack frame.

At most of the lakes included in this book, the lake or stream generally provides the only sources of water. To prepare it for drinking, boil it for three to five minutes, or bring some sort of filtering system, available at any outdoor recreation store. The waters of Oregon's lakes are quite pure, but even swiftly

Some of the boating equipment for backpackers: combination life and fishing vest, backpacker's fishing rod, inflatable raft or kayak, collapsible paddles, foot pump, and patch kit.

running mountain stream water is a potential carrier of giardia (a bacterium that can mess up your intestinal system in no time).

The sketch maps included in the text are intended to provide a general outline of the lake and surrounding roads and trails. The map of the national forest (listed in the heading of each lake) will give a more complete picture of where the lake is located and how to get there. The U.S. Geological Survey topographic maps (or topos) are the most detailed maps available, showing topographic contours and elevations as well as roads, trails, and streams. The appendix at the back of the book lists the major lakes and the U.S.G.S. topographic quadrangles in which the lakes can be found. Most specialty backpacking stores carry topos, as do some larger libraries with map rooms.

A Note on The Care and Treatment of Oregon's Wilderness

It is the moral responsibility of all people who venture into Oregon's natural areas to leave them as they were found—if only to preserve the experience for the next time, for the next traveller.

Many of the lakes included in this book lie within the boundaries of designated wilderness areas. These areas come under specific regulations that limit the impact people can have on the environment in order to keep these places truly wild. The Forest Service urges that in these areas, especially, we practice no-trace camping.

Here are some tips from the U.S. Forest Service on "Without A Trace" camping:

1. Plan ahead: avoid holidays and weekends (you'll have a more solitary experience, and the lake will receive far less impact); use a campstove rather than building fires to cook; take a litter bag to carry out refuse—yours and whatever else you can carry out. Even developed campgrounds to which you can drive often provide no waste receptacles, so take all refuse away with you; never throw trash into the pit toilets.

2. Help maintain the trails you use: drain puddles, kick out rocks; walk single-file in the center of the trail; never shortcut switchbacks (that causes erosion of the trail); stay on the main trail even if it's wet or boggy.

3. Make no-trace camps: choose well-drained, needle-strewn or sandy campsites; avoid leveling or digging drainage ditches; wear lightweight, soft shoes around camp to avoid trampling vegetation.

4. When building fires, make them small; use existing fire rings; gather downed, small firewood from timbered areas outside the camp area; stir ashes with water, hand test, then sprinkle or bury the ashes.

5. Be protective of the water's purity: camp at least 200 feet from water sources; bury human waste and fish entrails six inches deep and at least 200 feet from drainage areas, campsites, or trails (bury toilet tissue with human waste); brush teeth and wash, using biodegradable soaps, and dispose of waste water at least 200 feet from water sources.

6. Help keep quiet areas quiet: keep pets close at hand and under control;

Rowboats on Clear Lake

camp as quietly as possible so that others may also savor the solitude (sounds travel remarkably well across the water's surface).

7. Be a leader: pick up and pack out all litter and non-burnables; erase all signs of a fire; replace rocks and logs where they were.

8. Spread the word: tell others about no-trace camping ethics and encourage them to help preserve Oregon's natural beauty.

Location of Major Lakes

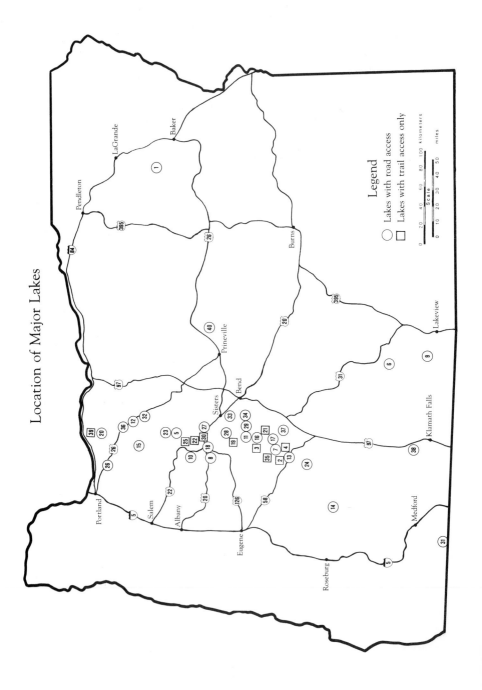

Legend

○ Lakes with road access
□ Lakes with trail access only

Map Key & Site Information

1. Anthony Lakes
2. Betty Lake
3. Blow & Doris Lakes
4. Bobby Lake
5. Breitenbush Lake
6. Campbell & Dead Horse
7. Charlton Lake
8. Clear Lake
9. Cottonwood Meadow Lake
10. Daly & Parrish Lakes
11. Devils Lake
12. Frog Lake
13. Gold Lake
14. Hemlock Lake
15. Hideaway Lake
16. Hosmer Lake
17. Irish & Taylor Lakes
18. Link Creek Basin Lakes
19. Linton Lake
20. Lost Lake

21. Lucky Lake
22. Marion Lake
23. Olallie Lake
24. Opal & Timpanogas Lakes
25. Pamelia Lake
26. Roslyn Lake
27. Round Lake
28. Scott Lake
29. Sparks Lake
30. Square Lake
31. Squaw Lakes
32. Summit Lake
33. Three Creeks Lake
34. Todd Lake
35. Torrey Lake
36. Trillium Lake
37. Twin Lake
38. Upper Klamath Lake
39. Wahtum Lake
40. Walton Lake

Key to Symbols

- Rough Road Access
- Trail Access Only
- Good Road Access
- Developed Campground
- Toilets
- Tables
- Drinking Water
- Fishing
- Boat Ramp
- Walking Trails
- Swimming
- Boat Rentals
- Groceries & Supplies
- Restaurant
- Cabin Rentals
- Showers
- Guard Station

21

1
Anthony Lakes

Baker County
Wallowa-Whitman National Forest
Distance from LaGrande: 45 miles

Probably one of the most scenic lakes in this part of the state, Anthony Lake affords inspiring views of the craggy Elkhorn Mountains rising to the south. Lookout Peak, Angel Peak, or Gunsight Mountain usually find their way into photographs from Anthony.

Rimmed by a forest of lodgepole pine, Engleman spruce, and subalpine fir, Anthony Lake is lovely even without the mountains. In winter the site of a popular ski resort, by the Fourth of July, Anthony Lake opens for camping, canoeing and rowboating, picnicking, and—for the very brave—swimming. Usually referred to in the plural, the area incorporates Anthony Lake and several smaller lakes nearby.

The Forest Service and the Oregon State Marine Board, in a move to protect the lake from pollution and noise, have prohibited gasoline-powered motors on Anthony. To preserve the recreational experience for handicapped individuals and senior citizens, however, small electric motors may be used.

The lake draws a considerable number of visitors during its short season—usually from July 4th through Labor Day. On weekends the campground averages 80 percent full. A fee campground sits on a knoll overlooking the north side of the lake. It contains 38 units, complete with running water and garbage containers, and a boat ramp on the east side of the lake next to the campground.

Six hike-in sites remain from the old campground on the south side, away from the lake. The marshy southern shore makes access to these campsites by boat impractical. Hikers will find the sites by walking west from the end of the road at either side of the lake.

A privately run resort currently offers rustic cabins and rowboats for rent. The small store stocks groceries and supplies, and there's a small cafe if you decide it's too cold to cook breakfast at camp. The resort will be dismantled by 1990 as part of the effort to reduce heavy recreation impact on the lake's fragile shoreline.

The 24-acre lake generally provides consistent fishing throughout the season for stocked rainbow and native Eastern brook trout. The rainbows run eight to 12 inches, and the brookies average six to 10. Popular methods include fly fishing and bank fishing with bait. Paved trails and fishing platforms make the lake handicap-accessible.

Those who like to mix a boating trip with good hiking will find much to

Photograph courtesy of the U.S. Forest Service

occupy them at Anthony Lakes. Maps are available from the Guard Station at the lake. The Elkhorn Crest National Recreation Trail (No. 1611) begins here and follows the crest of the Elkhorn Mountains 24 miles to a point on the Elkhorn Crest overlooking Baker and Sumpter Valley. It sounds like an endurance test, but once you reach the top, the trail follows a fairly even grade.

Other trails include an easy one-mile hike to Black Lake on the rebuilt Trail No. 1600 and a more difficult mile due south to Hoffer Lakes on Trail No. 1641. Older but well-maintained, the Hoffer Lakes Trail climbs a steeper grade. Bring your fishing gear and cast for the rainbow or brook trout to be found in each of these lakes.

The trail to Crawfish Lake takes off about five miles beyond the campground from Forest Road 73, roughly 1¼ miles into the 15-acre lake, where the brookies are small but plentiful.

Van Patten Lake lies about a mile south of Forest Road 73 via Trail No. 1634. The trail takes off about two miles east of the Anthony Lake Guard Station (where you can obtain maps of area trails and other information). The lake remains a favorite for anglers because of the consistently good trout fishing throughout the season. The fingerlings stocked here bi-annually grow up to 14 inches.

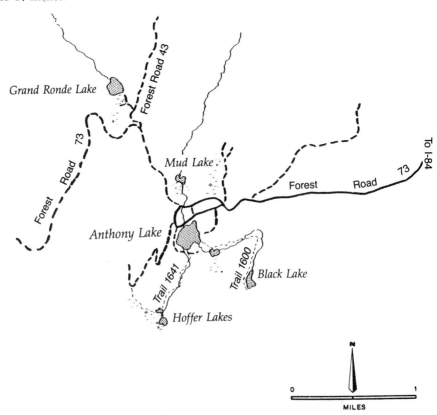

You can drive to Grand Ronde Lake, about a mile north of Anthony on Forest Road 43. Mud Lake lies directly north across road 73 from Anthony Lake, but you have to walk in a short distance. Grand Ronde harbors stocked rainbow, and both lakes have native populations of brook trout. Because the road ends before it reaches Mud Lake, it provides no access to motor boats; Grand Ronde Lake carries the same limits to motors as Anthony Lake.

To get to the Anthony Lakes area, take Interstate 84 to North Powder (located between LaGrande and Baker) and drive west about 20 miles, following signs to Highway 411 and Anthony Lakes Ski Resort. Highway 411 becomes Forest Road 73, which leads to the lake.

2
Betty Lake

Lane County
Willamette National Forest
Distance from Eugene: 68 miles

Situated an easy ½-mile off Waldo Lake Road in the Willamette National Forest, Betty Lake is surprisingly undisturbed. A small lake surrounded by forest and complete with rainbow trout averaging a nice 10 inches, it affords a taste of the backcountry just off the road. At least one pair of tiny Goldeneye ducks frequents the waters of Betty Lake.

The short hike makes it possible to portage a canoe into this 40-acre lake, although it's small enough to get around easily in an inflatable. The fish bite well on bait and lures, and fly fishing can be productive in the early morning and early evening. The mosquitoes bite well, too, especially in late spring, so bring plenty of repellent.

Betty Lake offers no developed campsites, but you'll find several natural spots, including one on an island-like peninsula that enters the lake from the southwest shore. The sandy bottom in this area makes it nice for swimming later in summer.

If you want a less rustic camping experience, you could drive a few miles farther to one of Waldo Lake's sophisticated campgrounds (complete with flushies) as a base camp from which to explore several of the lakes in this area. See separate entries for Bobby Lake, Charlton Lake, Gold Lake, Irish and Taylor Lakes, and Torrey and Wahanna Lakes.

A great place for children—just an easy half-mile from the car and forgotten supplies—Betty Lake has several shallow areas for swimming and a tiny lake next to it that can be fun for wading. You can see the smaller lake from the road, but you have to walk overland to get to it—not difficult because the area has very little undergrowth.

For hikers, a trail circles Betty Lake and continues north to Howkum, Horsefly, and Tiny Lakes, within a mile beyond; about three miles will take you to Shadow Bay on Waldo Lake.

To get to Betty Lake, take State Highway 58 about 23 miles southeast of Oakridge to Forest Road 5897, signed to Waldo Lake. The trailhead lies about five miles beyond, on the west side of the road. At 5,500-foot elevation, the lake usually becomes accessible in June.

Betty Lake

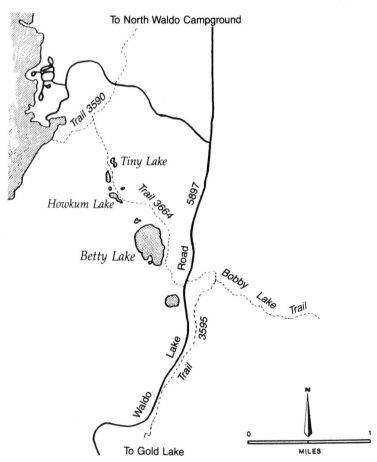

To North Waldo Campground

Trail 3590

$\mathcal{S}$ *Tiny Lake*

Trail 3664

5897

Howkum Lake

Betty Lake

Road

Bobby Lake Trail

3595

Waldo Lake Trail

To Gold Lake

N

0   1

MILES

27

3
Blow & Doris Lakes

Deschutes County
Deschutes National Forest
Distance from Bend: 37 miles

Hikers often pass Blow Lake by on their way into the Mink Lake Basin, which leaves this a quiet spot for boaters who wish to stay for the night. The short walk across even terrain also makes this is an ideal day trip. Horse campers use this trail on their way to the backcountry but rarely stop here.

You'll find several primitive campsites around the 45-acre lake, but no developments. Or you could camp at nearby Elk Lake, which has a developed campground, then hike in to Blow Lake to get away from the crowds often found at the larger lake.

Stocked brook trout in Blow Lake average around 10 inches. Try your luck off the lava flow on the west side, across from where the trail reaches the lake. Fishing probably peaks in June, but fall anglers also fare well.

By July—or August for the warm-blooded—the water should be fine for swimming. The lake is a little over 20 feet at its deepest, so the Central Oregon sun warms it sooner than others.

If you continue past Blow Lake about a mile, you'll come to the larger Doris Lake. A beautiful blue lake with a picturesque view, Doris holds about 70 acres of water and hosts Eastern brook trout, stocked annually. Campers will find no developments, but several rustic campsites ring the lake, including some favorites on the south shore.

Although surrounded by hemlock and lodgepole pine, the lack of underbrush around these lakes allows you to explore them as easily on foot as by boat. Your inflatable will come in handy for fishing at Doris Lake because the deep waters—roughly 90 feet near the center—suggest trolling as an effective method. The shallower waters at the extreme western and eastern ends of the lake offer fair fly fishing during late fall especially. In mid- to late-summer, hikers don their swimming suits (or not) and take to these shallows for a swim.

Serious hikers might want to continue the trek west to encounter several lakes in the Mink Lake Basin. Most of these offer excellent fishing; Mink Lake is stocked annually with rainbow, brook, and cutthroat trout.

Supplies can be purchased nearby at the resorts of Elk Lake (two miles north) and Lava Lake (four miles south), both off Century Drive. To reach Blow Lake, take Cascade Lakes Highway 46 (Century Drive) from Bend about 37 miles. The Six Lakes Trail (No. 14) begins from a parking area on the west side about a mile south of Elk Lake. The trail climbs steeply at first, then gradually for about 1½ miles to Blow Lake.

Doris Lake

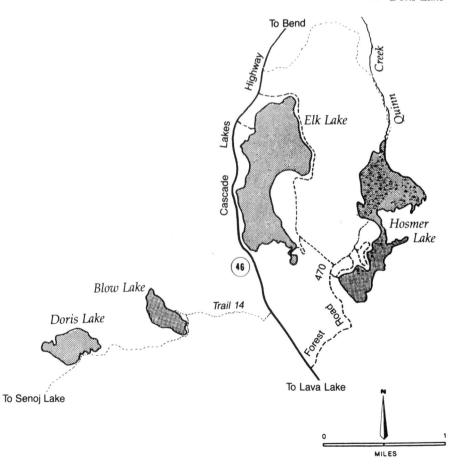

To Bend

Highway

Creek

Quinn

Cascade   Lakes

Elk Lake

Hosmer
Lake

46

470

Blow Lake

Doris Lake

Trail 14

Forest   Road

To Senoj Lake

To Lava Lake

N

0   1

MILES

4
Bobby Lake

Deschutes County
Deschutes National Forest
Distance from Eugene: 68 miles

This beautiful lake was a real discovery for us. Good-sized at 91 acres, Bobby receives only light recreational use, despite easy trail access and good fishing. The 2½-mile walk passes quickly, taking you through dense forest along an even, well-maintained trail.

Fishing alone makes it well worth the trip, with brook trout sometimes taken up to 16 inches. (They average around 10.) You might try casting a few flies in the shallow water from the center into the east arm. Trolling with bait or lures will be more productive in the west arm, where the water depth near the center reaches nearly 60 feet.

You'll find several primitive campsites, primarily on the south shore. With no inlet streams and an intermittent outlet stream on the east end, the lake serves as the only water source.

The lake's eastern edge offers a spectacular vantage point for a picnic—atop a large outcropping of rock. The sandy floor and shallow water here also make this spot nice for swimming.

The area around Bobby Lake provides ample opportunity for hiking, as well. The Pacific Crest National Scenic Trail (PCT) intersects the Bobby Lake Trail, which you take from the Waldo Lake Road (Forest Road 5897), about ½ mile west of Bobby Lake. You can walk the PCT north approximately six miles to Charlton Lake, or turn south for 4½ miles to reach Gold Lake (see separate entries). Continuing east past Bobby Lake another six miles on Moore Creek Trail will take you to Davis Lake.

To reach Bobby Lake, take Oregon Highway 58 southeast from Oakridge to the Waldo Lake Road, Forest Road 5897, and drive north about 5½ miles to the Bobby Lake trailhead (on the east side of the road). You can park across the road at the Betty Lake trailhead, which has a wider shoulder for cars. The nearest supplies are in Oakridge, about 35 miles, and at Crescent Junction, about 10 miles to the southeast.

Bobby Lake

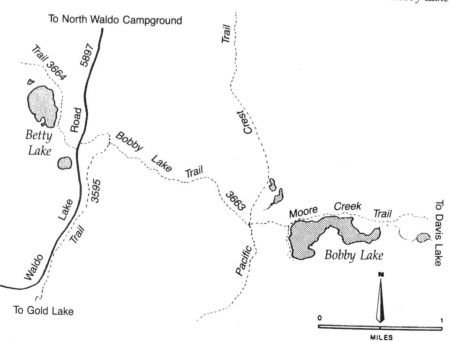

To North Waldo Campground

Trail 3664

5897

Betty Lake

Road

Bobby Lake Trail

Trail

Crest

3663

Waldo Lake Trail 3595

Pacific

Moore Creek Trail

Bobby Lake

To Davis Lake

To Gold Lake

N

0   MILES   1

5
Breitenbush Lake

Clackamas County
Mt. Hood National Forest
Distance from Portland: 85 miles

Nestled within the boundaries of the Warm Springs Indian Reservation and the Olallie Lakes Scenic Area, Breitenbush Lake lies at the foot of Campbell Butte at 5,500 feet. You'll want a high-clearing vehicle to travel the rough and rocky road to get there. But the scenery—a breathtaking view of Mt. Jefferson, the surrounding forested foothills and high mountain meadows, the wildflowers, and the clear water of the lake—makes it worth the bumpy ride.

The 65-acre lake holds native brook and rainbow trout, as well as stocked trout, and at times you can enjoy excellent fishing. Fly fishing works particularly well in the shallows (nearly three-quarters of the lake has a depth of less than 10 feet), with August and September offering the best results. Fishing permits from the Confederated Tribes of Warm Springs have generally not been required. For current information, call (503) 553-1161.

A campground with 20 sites, run by the U.S. Forest Service for the Confederated Tribes of Warm Springs, sits at the edge of a large alpine meadow on the western shore. The lake provides the only water source, but the campground has pit toilets and two small log shelters. You can launch your boat here, but the reeds and shallow water, navigable by canoe or kayak, can be tricky in a cartop or inflatable.

A sandy beach on the north shore makes a great spot for an afternoon picnic in view of Mt. Jefferson. You can wade in the shallow water or swim if the water's to your liking. Be careful, though, of the northwest shore, which drops off fairly rapidly.

Hikers can have a great time exploring the many smaller lakes in this glaciated basin. The Pacific Crest National Scenic Trail (PCT) passes within ¼ mile of Breitenbush Lake, and Gibson Lake Trail (No. 708) skirts the western shore, leading north to Gibson Lake before joining the PCT. The Olallie Guard Station, five miles north of Breitenbush on Oregon Skyline Road 4220, provides maps of the area's lakes and trails.

Two routes will take you to Breitenbush Lake. From State Highway 26, turn south on Forest Road 42 for about 27 miles to Forest Road 4220 (Oregon Skyline Road), following signs to Olallie Lake. Continue past Olallie Lake on the Skyline Road about five miles beyond the Guard Station. For an aerial view of Olallie and Monon Lakes, stop at the second switchback south of Horseshoe Lake. The last two miles follow a rocky, primitive road that can be especially tricky if it's wet or raining.

Breitenbush Lake & Mt. Jefferson

From Detroit Reservoir, take Forest Road 46 northeast along the North Fork of the Breitenbush River until you reach Road 4220. From here, it's about eight rugged miles to the lake.

The nearest source of supplies, including gasoline and a limited range of fishing tackle, is the Olallie Lake Resort, about six miles north along Skyline Road (see Olallie Lake entry).

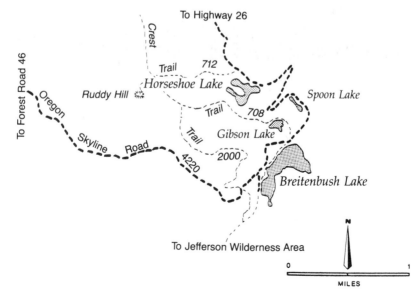

33

6
Campbell &
Dead Horse Lakes

Klamath County
Fremont National Forest
Distance from Lakeview: 47 miles

A forest of lodgepole pine encircles these two remote high-elevation lakes in an area of few natural lakes. A little more than a mile apart, both lakes provide a haven for serene boating and good fishing.

Fifteen campsites ring Campbell Lake, where facilities include tables and grills, with one water pump located about half-way around the circle. A boat ramp lies on the north end of the lake, just off the day-use picnic area.

At Dead Horse, 10 campsites rest along the shore near where the road reaches the lake, and another three can only be reached by boat directly across from the day-use area. Another eight units sit ¼ mile above the lake.

These lakes both receive a lot of pressure from anglers; in fact, most visitors come just for the fishing. Holiday weekends find the campgrounds filled to capacity, but other weekends through the short season (mid-July to late September or mid-October) also draw activity.

Legal-sized rainbows are stocked annually in each, and Dead Horse Lake has a reproducing population of Eastern brook trout. The average size is around 10 to 12 inches. Anglers most often troll spinners and lures.

Fed by snowmelt, and at nearly 7,200-foot elevation, the lake water always runs cold and very clear. As for wildlife, you might see an occasional deer or elk, and osprey work these lakes for their meals.

If you want to enjoy a hike one day rather than fish, Dead Horse Trail takes you due south up onto Dead Horse Rim. The trail begins at Dead Horse Lake campground and loops around 11.4 miles to end at Lee Thomas campground along the North Fork of the Sprague River. The Fremont National Forest map doesn't show this trail, but maps are available at the Paisley, Bly, or Lakeview Ranger District offices.

To reach these isolated lakes from Paisley, drive southwest on Forest Road 331 about 23 miles, then south on Forest Road 2823 to Road 3403, which leads to Campbell Lake and another 1¼ miles to Dead Horse. From Bly, drive northeast approximately 35 miles to Forest Road 331 and turn left (west), following the directions above. The nearest supplies are in Paisley and Bly.

Photograph courtesy of the U.S. Forest Service

Campbell Lake

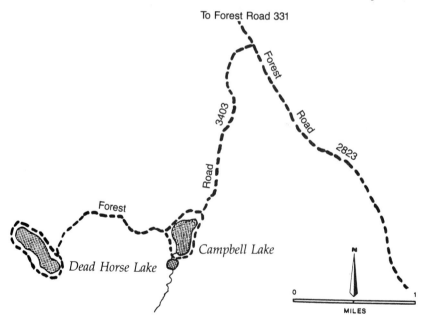

To Forest Road 331

Forest

Road

3403

Road

2823

Forest

Dead Horse Lake

Campbell Lake

N

0   MILES   1

7
Charlton Lake

Deschutes County
Deschutes National Forest
Distance from Eugene: 73 miles

Charlton Lake rests almost on the crest of the Cascade Mountains, at the edge of the Deschutes National Forest. It holds 156 acres of pure, blue water— as well as some large but fairly elusive brook trout.

The lake's irregular shape and deep, clear waters make Charlton a natural for canoeists, and since the lake lies only about 100 yards from the road, you could portage a canoe, kayak, or cartop. These might be more practical for getting around on a lake this size than an inflatable raft.

Charlton receives relatively few visitors, considering its accessibility and attractive setting. But those who do come have taken care to preserve it by camping in the Forest Service campsites rather than blazing new ones, and by packing out everything they bring in.

If you'd like more comforts to your camping (you'll find no developments at Charlton), you could set up a base at either Islet or North Waldo, two fully equipped campgrounds on Waldo Lake, just a few miles to the west.

The lake provides the only water source, and the water quality is excellent (but always boil before drinking). At nearly 5,700 feet elevation, the water is also quite cold. Sitting near the mountain summit often means strong winds, which can make the waters of Charlton pretty choppy. If the winds whip up, stay close to the shoreline.

For hikers, the trail skirts the southern shore, heading toward Found Lake, about 2½ miles to the south. Or take the Pacific Crest National Scenic Trail north about six miles to Irish and Taylor Lakes (see separate entry).

Fishing at Charlton can be good, but its size can make the brookies harder to find. Fly anglers will have their best luck in early morning and around dusk later in the season, keeping to the shallower waters in the southeastern corner of the lake's west arm. Trolling with lures or spinners will also bring success.

If you can stand it, you might enjoy swimming in the height of summer, when the fishing sometimes slackens. You can also just kick back and drink in the beautiful scenery. Whatever you do, bring plenty of mosquito repellent, especially if you come early in the season.

Once extremely remote, Charlton can now be reached via paved roads, with the exception of about ½ mile of gravel. Charlton Lake lies just off Waldo Lake Road, just south of the North Waldo Lake turnoff. To get there, take Highway 58 southeast from Oakridge to the Waldo Lake Road, Forest

Charlton Lake

Road 5897. The road to Charlton, also 5897, turns east about 12 miles north-east of Hwy 58. It's about ½ mile to where you have to park along the road and walk the last 100 yards to the lake. The nearest supplies and gasoline can be found at Crescent Junction, about 13 miles southeast, or in Oakridge, some 38 miles to the west.

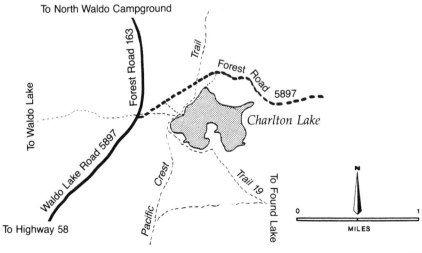

8
Clear Lake

Linn County
Willamette National Forest
Distance from Corvallis: 80 miles

This lake, in many ways, was the inspiration for this entire book. We've been settling our canoe into the pristine waters of Clear Lake for many years now, and we've never tired of the thrill of quietly paddling along its shore; we've never ceased to marvel at how *clear* the waters of Clear Lake truly are; and we've especially appreciated being able to "hear" the silence of gliding the canoe over the glassy calm of the lake at dusk.

But we're not the only ones. The years have brought many developments to Clear Lake, making it more accessible and therefore more popular. Midsummer weekends find Clear Lake full to the brim, and if you want to stay in one of the small resort cabins on a weekend, you'd better book it months in advance. On weekends earlier in the season and midweek days you can still capture a choice campsite, but many of the near-shore sites are reserved for handicapped campers until six p.m. daily.

Coldwater Cove, a well-developed fee campground on the southeastern shore, has facilities including pit toilets and refuse containers, picnic tables, cook stands and fire rings, and sweet, pure spring water from several old-fashioned red pumps. We often bottle some Clear Lake water for the trip home, but nothing can beat getting it straight and cold from the pump.

Clear Lake Resort, at the northwest end of the lake, rents several rustic but reasonably priced cabins equipped with heater, gas stove, and electric lights (turned on during peak evening hours only; kerosene lamps are available for night owls). Bring your own bed linen and blankets. Some deluxe cabins have showers and in-house privies. If you aren't into cooking for yourself, the small cafe serves breakfast, lunch, and dinner, and your sweet tooth will savor the breakfast rolls and pies baked fresh every day.

Rowboats can be rented by the hour or by the day, and the resort carries a limited supply of fishing tackle for sale. You might also glean some good advice about fishing over a cup of coffee.

The fishing in Clear Lake ranges from hot to just plain awful, but those who work at it throughout the day can usually catch their limit. The photos in the lodge will attest that some trophy-sized trout have been taken from the lake's deep waters.

Stocked regularly with rainbow trout, Clear Lake also supports a reproducing population of brook trout. This lake definitely has good and bad times of day to be fishing, though. The hottest hours begin just after dawn and last until the sun comes over the ridge, then again within about half an hour of dusk. Later in the morning, keep to the shadows and you might fare well. All methods will catch fish, but many anglers favor trolling with bait and flashers or still-fishing with marshmallows. Flies generally work well nearer the out-let—the McKenzie river gets its start at the southwest corner of the lake. A sign warns of the fast water ahead, but the roar of the McKenzie rushing over massive basalt boulders usually sounds warning enough.

Clear Lake was formed when Little Nash Crater erupted some 3,000 years ago. The lava dammed the river that flowed through the valley, covering the

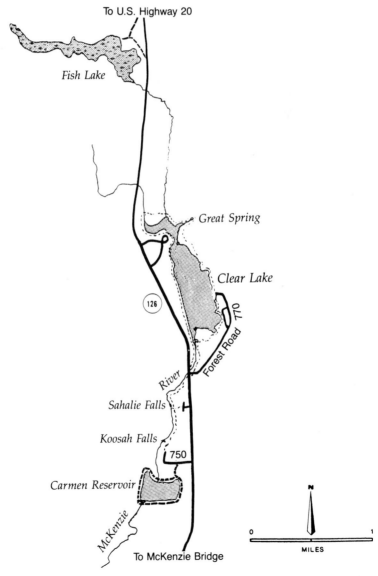

forest with water that now reaches a depth of more than 200 feet. You can still see many of the trees on the lake floor. The trees aren't petrified, but because of the icy temperature of the water, they haven't fully decomposed.

Great or Big Spring, at the northeast corner of the lake, is a magical spot. Early in the season the water flows out high enough that you can paddle a canoe upstream into the large pool, charged with an iridescent blue, a cool reminder of its temperature. The spring water flows into the lake at around 33 degrees, helping maintain an average temperature of 34 to 38 degrees in the lake year round. The extremely clear water has made Clear Lake popular with scuba divers, but wetsuits are a must!

Midday, when there's a lull in the fishing action, is the perfect time for a walk. You can circle the lake on a well-blazed trail, newly linked by bridges over the McKenzie and Ikenick Creek; in all you'll follow about 5½ miles of trail around the lake. Or take the McKenzie River National Recreation Trail, which you can meet by walking southwest from the campground, and follow the powerful McKenzie about a mile to where it roars over a towering cliff of volcanic basalt. Sahalie Falls, which means "high" in Chinook Indian jargon, drops 100 feet, spraying a fine mist to cool onlookers. Walk just above the viewpoint at the top of the falls to view a breathtaking series of smaller falls, where the waters of the McKenzie churn an icy bluegreen.

Two other lakes nearby provide additional opportunities for recreation as well as overflow for camping when Coldwater Cove fills with campers.

Two miles to the south, Carmen Reservoir lies along the McKenzie River. Although not in as pretty a setting as Clear Lake, this 65-acre reservoir does offer fairly good fishing, and the campground—adjacent to dazzling Koosah Falls on the McKenzie—isn't nearly as crowded. You'll find most of the out-door conveniences at the Ice Cap Creek Campground serving Carmen, but you'll pay a nightly fee.

Just about two miles north of Clear Lake you'll find Fish Lake—but only if you arrive early in the season. By August, the lake has virtually dried up. Before fishing season for this lake ends May 31, Fish Lake does offer fair angling for cutthroat trout, ranging in size from six to 14 inches. There's usu-ally enough water for paddling around through June, and it's a good place for watching waterfowl. But beware—as the water drains into Clear Lake over the summer, all those mosquito larvae that have been underwater begin to hatch. The semi-developed campground at Fish Lake is free of charge.

To reach Clear Lake Resort, take Highway 20 east about 70 miles from Interstate 5 to the junction with State Highway 126. Drive south about four miles, then turn left at the signed road to the resort, about a mile. The campground is 1¼ miles farther south on Highway 126. A free boat ramp is available at the campground; you can launch boats at the resort for a small fee.

For reservations at the resort, write well in advance for a brochure from the Santiam Fish & Game Association, P.O. Box 95, Sweet Home, Oregon 97386.

9
Cottonwood
Meadow Lake

Lake County
Fremont National Forest
Distance from Lakeview: 28 miles

This small, spring-fed reservoir, unlike the larger Cottonwood Reservoir about eight miles downstream, is a non-motor lake with several improvements for recreational use. Forests of ponderosa pine and white fir border three sides of Cottonwood Meadow Lake, but the late 1970's brought a large forest fire to the northwest edge of the lake.

An earthen dam across Cottonwood Creek created the lake in 1961. Since then, it has been stocked with rainbow and brook trout, and the rainbow fingerlings currently stocked grow well in the nutrient-rich waters. The lake receives lots of fishing activity, especially early in the season. Just about any method will catch fish, although many locals prefer fly angling. Later in the summer the fishing slackens as the algae bloom comes on. A walking trail circles the lake, so a boat isn't necessary for fishing, but it is helpful. You can put in at the boat ramp near the campground.

A good-sized campground sits on the east side of the lake. Facilities include tables, fire rings, outhouses, and running water. Holiday and early-season weekends usually find the campground filled.

The route to the lake follows good road all the way in. From Lakeview, take State Highway 140 about 20 miles to Forest Road 387 and turn north, about five miles to the lake. The nearest supplies are in Lakeview or in Bly, 22 miles northwest.

Photograph courtesy of Portland State University, Geography Dept. Cottonwood Meadow Lake

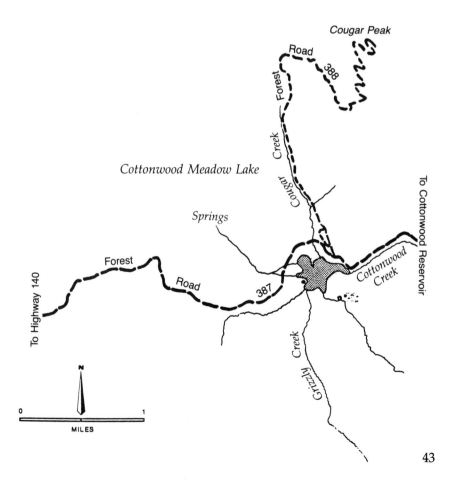

Cougar Peak

Road

Forest

388

Cottonwood Meadow Lake

Cougar Creek

Springs

To Cottonwood Reservoir

Forest

Road

387

Cottonwood Creek

To Highway 140

Grizzly Creek

N

0   1
MILES

10
Daly & Parrish Lakes

Linn County
Willamette National Forest
Distance from Portland: 127 miles

Daly Lake is one of those lakes we almost decided not to share. We renamed it Honeymoon Lake because that was our first encounter with it. We found it accidentally after a snowbank kept us from our original destination in the Olallie Lakes Scenic Area. We saw the blue spot on the map and decided to give it a try. So it's a very special lake—take good care of it.

Daly Lake sits nestled in a broad conifer forest, about 150 yards off the road. The short walk allows for portaging a canoe or cartop, and the 11-acre lake offers pretty fair fishing for brook and cutthroat trout, considering its size. It's a quiet spot, except for the beautiful stream rushing into it at the southwest shore. A few rustic campsites and a pit toilet provide the only improvements at the lake. Two sites lie perched on a knoll relatively near the stream, which provides an invigorating natural symphony. From the "front porch" of our tent we looked out on the bluegreen lake. The rest of the terrain around the lake is steep enough to preclude pitching a tent.

We enjoyed several encounters with wildlife at Daly Lake. In the evening, three black-tail deer stopped by to check out our campfire. In the early morning hours and just after dusk, keep an eye out for a couple of very busy beavers—you can see their handiwork among the trees all around the shore, and they've built a small dam at one end of the lake.

A mile-long maintained trail circles Daly Lake, and following the stream beds can also prove interesting, especially when they disappear underground and you find them again several yards beyond.

Just down the road a spell is the trail to Parrish Lake. A bit smaller at around seven acres, it, too, offers fair fishing for natural brook trout. As with Daly, it's just a short walk from the road, and you'll find no improved sites but good natural spots for camping and one outhouse.

To reach these lakes, take State Highway 22 east past Detroit Reservoir, then drive south about eight miles past the Marion Forks Guard Station to Forest Road 2266 and turn west. (Or take State Highway 20 east toward Santiam Pass, turning north at the junction with Highway 22. It's about seven miles to Forest Road 2266.) Follow 2266 to the junction with spur road 450 and turn north (right) about ¼ mile to Daly Lake, or south (left) about the same distance to Parrish Lake. You can't see the lakes from the road, but the trailheads are signed.

The nearest supplies are at Clear Lake Resort, 20 miles southwest, or Idanha, 21 miles north.

Daly Lake from the tent window

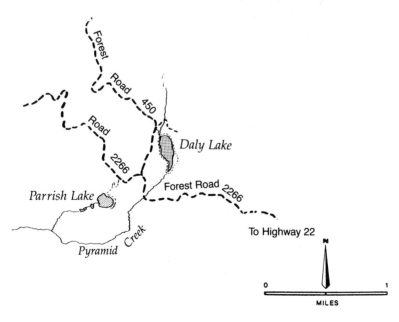

45

11
Devils Lake

Deschutes County
Deschutes National Forest
Distance from Bend: 30 miles

One of many picturesque lakes along Century Drive west of Bend, Devils Lake is distinctive because of its remarkable color—a turquoise blue that makes you wonder if one of the goddesses lost a gem. The extremely clear water sparkles over the white pumice bottom, less than 10 feet from the surface at its deepest. Often folks traveling the Cascade Lakes Highway stop just to look at it (Devils is one of the few lakes that can be seen from the highway).

Tent-dwellers willing to walk their gear a short distance from the parking area will find some lovely campsites overlooking the lake. Boats, too, must be walked in, as there is no boat ramp. You'll hear no motor boats on the 23-acre lake, but because of Devils' proximity to the highway, you can hear the cars go by easily enough.

The semi-developed, tent-only camp area has no water source besides the lake. If all the sites are taken, or if you'd like a few more creature comforts, Elk Lake, about four miles to the south, offers a resort and a more developed campground.

Anglers will find natural brook trout and stocked rainbow in Devils Lake, but catching them in this extremely clear, shallow water can be a challenge. Experts suggest using very light leader. Fly anglers will have fair luck before and after the sun hits the lake, especially if a breeze ruffles the surface.

This is a good lake for children, too. The campsites are away from the road, and although the glacier-fed lake never warms much over the summer, its shallow shores can be fine for wading.

Hikers will find lots to explore here. Many climbers use this as a base camp for heading up South Sister. Others hike in to 12-acre Moraine Lake, about two miles north via trails 36 and 17. Although it probably has no fish after being frozen solid all winter, Moraine Lake offers a spectacular view of South Sister. You'll find several natural spots to pitch your tent, but no improvements.

To reach Devils Lake, drive southwest from Bend on Century Drive (Cascade Lakes Highway 46). The lake lies along the south side of the highway about 30 miles from Bend.

Photograph courtesy of Portland State University, Geography Dept.

Devils Lake

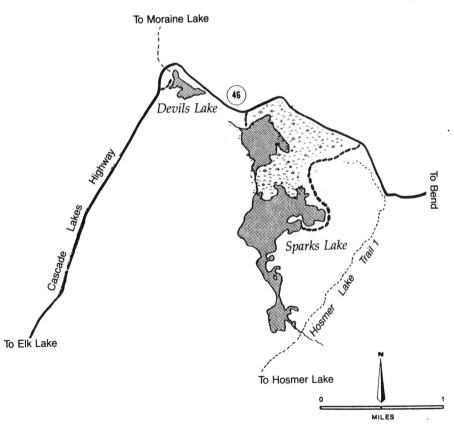

To Moraine Lake

46

Devils Lake

Cascade Lakes Highway

To Bend

Sparks Lake

Hosmer Lake Trail 1

To Elk Lake

To Hosmer Lake

N

0   1

MILES

12
Frog Lake

Clackamas County
Mt. Hood National Forest
Distance from Portland: 60 miles

This shallow lake on the south slopes of Mt. Hood gets shallower toward the end of the summer, but don't expect to find hundreds of frogs lining its shores. Nearly a dozen Frog Lakes dot the Oregon landscape, but the name for this particular one remains a mystery. Perhaps when the first pioneers or surveyors camped at the lake they were serenaded by frogs that have since moved on.

This sunny lake has a nice view of Mt. Hood to the north. The ducks living here know the meaning of rustling paper, and they'll appreciate it if you take along some extra bread.

Frog Lake gets extremely heavy recreational use, but surprisingly, during midweek you might find yourself among only a handful of campers. Camping in designated sites at the north end of the lake includes all the amenities—for a fee. There's also a boat ramp at the north shore and a picnic area along the southwest shore. A nice lake for families, the water gets rather warm toward late summer, and the sandy bottom allows children to wade easily along the shallow shoreline.

The lake is heavily fished for stocked rainbow—by late season you might as well forget the rod and just enjoy a good swim. Early in the season just about any method will bring in some pan-sized trout.

If you'd really like to fish—or are just interested in exploring—you might try hiking in to Twin Lakes, about 1½ miles north of Frog Lake. These lakes offer pretty fair fishing, although for hike-in lakes, they're heavily fished. The deeper waters help fish evade the catch a little more easily. Two routes lead into these lakes. The Pacific Crest National Scenic Trail crosses the road into Frog Lake about ½ mile from the lake at the north end of the snow park; walk north a little over a mile. Or take Trail No. 484 east from the campground about a mile, then north another 1½ miles. A primitive campground is maintained at the lower lake; the upper lake lies about ½ mile to the north.

To get to Frog Lake, take U.S. Highway 26 east toward Madras. About four miles south of its junction with State Highway 35, turn east (left) on Forest Road 2610, following signs through the snow park to the lake.

Frog Lake & Mt. Hood

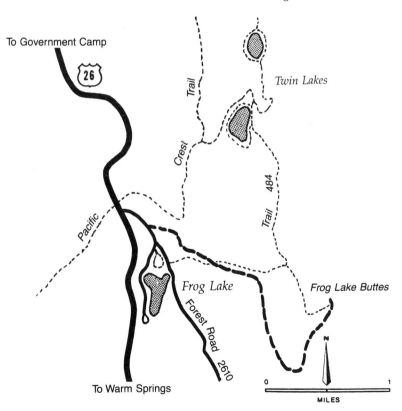

To Government Camp

26

Twin Lakes

Trail

Crest

Trail 484

Pacific

Frog Lake

Frog Lake Buttes

Forest Road 2610

To Warm Springs

0   N   1

MILES

13
Gold Lake

Lane County
Willamette National Forest
Distance from Eugene: 63 miles

Another very special place, quiet Gold Lake is nestled half in meadow, half in forest. You understand the meaning in the lake's name when the sun strikes the water at an oblique angle, casting a gold-green hue on the lake floor and setting small "flakes" in the water to sparkling. From the north end of the lake you can spy snow-capped Diamond Peak.

The large bog at the north end has been designated a Natural Research Area because it is rich with rare plants, including several carnivorous species. If you visit the area, walk softly on the bog and take nothing away with you but photographs and good memories.

Fly anglers number among the majority of visitors to Gold Lake, as fishing here is limited to fly tackle. The lake maintains natural populations of brook and rainbow trout, neither of which are currently stocked. The brush-lined and often boggy shores of this 96-acre lake make a boat part of the necessary fishing equipment. You can put in at the boat launch near the outlet stream. Two springs feed into the north end of the lake, where the shallow waters often harbor lots of fish. The streams themselves, as well as the outlet stream, are closed to fishing.

A developed Forest Service campground at the south end of the lake provides several pleasant sites at the lake's edge. You'll probably be visited by a family of mallards making the rounds of the campground for handouts. The jays—both gray and stellar's—and the chipmunks can be pretty bold, too. As you walk through the campground, keep your eyes open for some large snowshoe hares.

The fee campground has one water pump near the entrance, and tables and fire rings at each site. If the campground is full, you might find a couple of natural sites on the west and east shores by boat.

If the fishing slacks off here, you could try your luck at one of several other lakes in the area. Marilyn Lakes are nearest, about ½ mile south by trail from the campground. Both offer good fly fishing, with brook trout reaching 15 inches or better. You can walk to Island Lakes via the Island Lake Trail (No. 3674), about two miles west from the campground (walk to the end of the spur road to find the trail, which crosses Waldo Lake Road before continuing west). Fishing for brook trout peaks in late fall, but if it's fish you're after, you'll do well to stay at Gold Lake in that part of the season.

Gold Lake

The nearest supplies are at Odell and Crescent Lake resort areas, about seven to 10 miles to the southeast.

To reach Gold Lake, drive east from Oakridge on State Highway 58. Take the Gold Lake Road (spur road no. 500), about two miles beyond the Waldo Lake turnoff and just west of the Gold Lake Snow Park; drive two miles north to the campground on a single-lane gravel road. The lake is usually accessible by June.

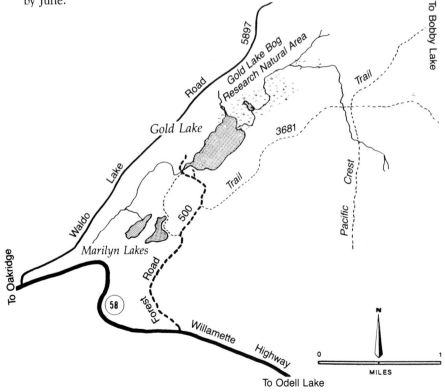

14
Hemlock Lake & Lake-in-the-Woods

Douglas County
Umpqua National Forest
Distance from Roseburg: 50 miles

More accessible than many of the lakes in this forest, Hemlock and Lake-in-the-Woods present a variety of experiences, from canoeing and fishing to wildflowers and waterfalls. Both are artificial lakes, but they look as if they've been around for millennia. The surrounding forests and meadows come alive with wildflowers and rhododendrons once snows have thawed, usually in late May or early June.

Hemlock, at around 28 acres, is the larger, and reaches a depth of 33 feet. Camping facilities include tables, fire places, outhouses, and garbage containers, but no developed water system. A boat ramp at Hemlock Meadows, ½ mile around the east arm of the lake, provides access to the lake.

Lake-in-the-Woods provides more comforts for a nightly fee in a slightly smaller campground, complete with wells for drinking water, flush toilets, tables, fire places, and garbage containers. The campsites lie along the road that circles the four-acre, eight-foot-deep lake.

Both lakes are stocked annually with fingerling rainbow, and Hemlock supports a reproducing population of kokanee salmon. Your boat will be useful for trolling slowly along the shorelines or just drifting with the breeze.

By July, the waters of Hemlock have usually warmed enough for swimming. The shallow, murky water of Lake-in-the-Woods blooms with algae as early as June, precluding swimming on this lake.

From the campground, you can take two different trails through old-growth Douglas fir to waterfalls on Little River and Hemlock Creek. To the north, Yakso Falls Trail 1519 leads ¾ mile to Yakso Falls, around 70 feet high. About ½ mile south of the campground via Trail No. 1520, Hemlock Creek tumbles more than 60 feet down Hemlock Falls.

A scenic trail (No. 1522-A) loops around Hemlock Lake, joining Yellow Jacket Loop Trail, No. 1522, at the campground. A 6½-mile loop, Yellow Jacket heads southwest through high-elevation timber and meadows, leading into Yellow Jacket Glade country and back to Hemlock Meadows. Another trail, No. 1526 (not shown on the map) leads to the top of Flat Rock, elevation 5,310.

To reach these lakes from Interstate 5 take exit 129, following State Highway 138 and signs to Glide. Drive southeast from Glide on Little River Road, County Route 17, 17 miles to Forest Road 27. Five miles more takes you to the

Lake-in-the-Woods

top of the pavement. Continue on gravel road for five miles to Lake-in-the-Woods, another five miles to Hemlock Lake. The nearest supplies are at Peel Store, 21 miles northwest of Lake-in-the-Woods.

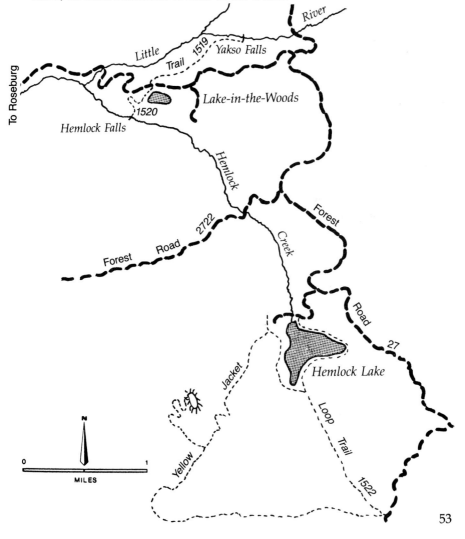

15
Hideaway Lake

Clackamas County
Mt. Hood National Forest
Distance from Portland: 68 miles

The headwaters of Shellrock Creek, which feeds into the Clackamas River, Hideaway Lake is not as inaccessible as its name might imply, yet it receives only light to moderate recreational use.

Once a hike-in lake, Hideaway now has several developed campsites, provided by the Autzen Foundation and the Izaak Walton League, complete with tables and fire rings, pit toilets, and occasionally running water.

The 12-acre, 30-foot-deep lake holds native brown trout as well as natural and stocked rainbow. Fly fishing can be productive in the shallower water especially, but bait and lures also work well. The earlier in the season you start, the better, although at 4,500 feet, the lake cannot usually be reached until late May or early June. Check with the Clackamas Ranger District.

On the west side of the lake, Trail No. 700 leads north past Shellrock Lake (½ mile), a popular lake for brook trout fishing. From there you can take Trail 517 then Trail 512 (about 1½ miles) to Rock Lakes, or to Serene Lake, about a mile farther west. These lakes hold a variety of trout—brook, cutthroat, and rainbow.

When the fishing tapers off in the heat of the summer, you can enjoy a swim, though because of the elevation, the water might be a bit chilly.

If you're driving from Portland, the shortest route is probably through Estacada, following State Highway 224 along the Clackamas River past the Ripplebrook Ranger Station, turning east on Forest Road 57. After about eight miles, turn north (left) on Forest Road 58, about 3½ miles to Road 5830. Turn west (left) about seven miles along this steep gravel road to the lake.

From the Mt. Hood area, continue south on U.S. Highway 26 after its junction with State Highway 35, about 10 miles. Turn right on Forest Road 42, following it eight miles to Forest Road 57. Drive past the south end of Timothy Lake and cross the dam. Both roads 57 and 5810 turn west to join 58, roughly two miles south of the lake; 57 follows the Clackamas River for a more scenic route, but it's a little more bumpy. Route 5810 is longer, but a better road. From either road, turn north (right) on Forest Road 58, then left on 5830 to the lake.

Hideaway Lake

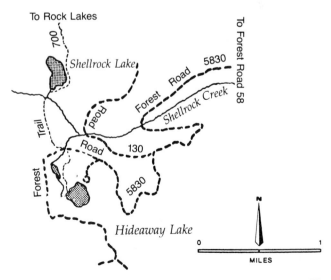

To Rock Lakes

Shellrock Lake

Forest Road 5830

Shellrock Creek

To Forest Road 58

Road

Trail

Road

130

Forest

5830

Hideaway Lake

N

0   1

MILES

16
Hosmer Lake

Deschutes County
Deschutes National Forest
Distance from Bend: 35 miles

Such an exceptional lake in so many ways, Hosmer deserves to be included in *Quiet Waters*, even though motorboats are allowed. Several restrictions on the use of motors, however, leave this lake relatively undisturbed. Motorboats cannot exceed the 10 mile per hour limit, and the motor cannot be running while fishing. The majority of visitors to Hosmer come for the fishing, and either they don't have motors or they use them simply to get from one spot to the next rather than as part of the recreational experience. Also, the shallow northern section of the lake presents the hazard of getting a motor stuck in the muddy bottom.

Hosmer holds so many little nooks and crannies to explore that it's easy to spend lots of time just boating, never mind the fish. But fishing is special here, too. Hosmer is the only lake west of the Mississippi River to support a population of landlocked Atlantic salmon, planted here in 1958. These beautiful silver-sided lunkers are wily—veterans of many battles with eager anglers. The lake is limited to fly fishing only (rod, reel, line, and flies) with barbless hooks (it's okay to pinch the barbs), and all Atlantic salmon must be released unharmed. Signs posted around the lake let you know how to tell the difference between the salmon and the brook trout, but if you tie into one of these, you'll probably know it. Some of the brook trout get quite large, too, because of the general catch-and-release practiced by a great many of the anglers who visit Hosmer. By releasing trout back into the lake, they hope to preserve this as the special place it is.

A long, narrow channel joins the two larger pools of the lake. To the east a small lava dam seeps water out of the lake, which is fed from the north by Quinn Creek. Silt has steadily been settling in Hosmer, and the encroaching vegetation will eventually turn this shallow lake into a large marsh.

Surrounded virtually on all sides by marshy reeds, Hosmer is best enjoyed by boat. A canoe lends itself especially well to exploring the more isolated and shallow north end. Hosmer also serves as a haven for wildlife. In the meadow surrounding the northern pool, you might chance upon deer, elk, or porcupine, among others. Playful otter and mink often glide through early morning waters. Bird watchers will find a variety of wildfowl, many nesting on the small islands that dot the northern half of the lake.

Two campgrounds rest on Hosmer's southwestern shore. Because of the reeds, access to the lake from either is difficult. However, a good boat ramp

Hungry gray jay at Hosmer Lake

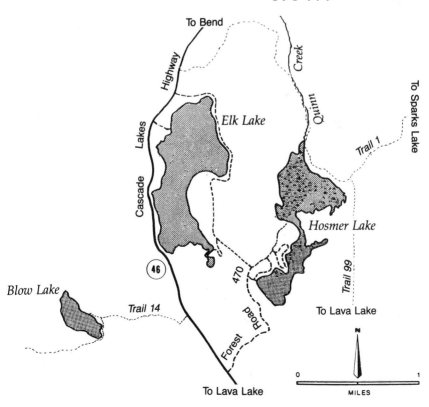

Hosmer Lake & South Sister

at the southern end of the lake provides both launch and access. Drinking water is no longer available because the well here turned sour.

Hosmer also affords magnificent vistas—Mt. Bachelor to the east and Three Sisters to the north, white-crested mountains rising above green meadows and forests. Camera buffs will want their macro lenses as well, with striking wildflowers abundant in the tall meadow grasses.

Take a break from fishing to explore Quinn Creek, which flows into the lake at its northwest point. Gliding upstream as far as the trail bridge, you may need to portage over a few log jams, but it's worth the effort. Or just dock the canoe alongside the stream and walk up; the ground is fairly firm here. As you progress, watch the water for the salmon that hunker in the shadows of fallen logs. If you bring your rod, it can be a real challenge getting one of these monsters to bite something—anything! Catching them with your bare hands might be easier (but don't try it—it's illegal).

If you want to check out more of the surrounding area, a hiking trail leads up the creek to Quinn Meadows, where several springs join to form Quinn Creek. It's pretty marshy, though, especially earlier in the season.

Hosmer is not a good swimming lake, both because of the shallow water (maximum depth 12 feet) and submerged vegetation. Also, any activity quickly stirs up the fine volcanic ash that covers the lake floor, muddying the otherwise crystal clear water. But don't let this deter you from visiting in the heat of summer—Elk Lake lies only a few miles up the road and offers plenty of opportunity for taking a dip.

To reach Hosmer, drive southwest from Bend approximately 35 miles on Century Drive (Cascade Lakes Highway 46). The turnoff to Hosmer is on the east (left) side of the road roughly one mile southeast of the last Elk Lake turnoff (Beach Campground). The nearest supplies and gasoline are at Elk Lake Resort, about three miles north.

17
Irish & Taylor Lakes

Deschutes County
Deschutes National Forest
Distance from Bend: 56 miles

These two remote lakes lie adjacent to one another along the road between Waldo and Cultus Lakes. Once the only means of getting to Waldo Lake, the difficult road access still means that Irish and Taylor Lakes remain quiet and secluded. They probably receive as much use from hikers passing through on the Pacific Crest National Scenic Trail as they do from motorists.

Camping at these lakes is primitive, although each has a backwoods privy (southeast corner of Irish, northeast shore of Taylor). One campsite at Taylor Lake, on a point at the northeast shore, can be driven to and has a picnic table. Most campsites lie near the road, and boat access for both lakes is for carried craft only.

The 5,000-foot elevation can make the evenings crisp, but the late summer sun warms both lakes enough for brisk daytime swims. For boating, Taylor's various arms and inlets make it the more interesting of the two because its whole isn't readily visible from any point—several fingers and bays wait to be investigated.

Fishing, however, is best at Irish Lake, which measures 35 acres and sports Eastern brook trout that grow to 16 inches or better. Taylor is larger and shallower, but holds fewer fish. On Irish, bait or lures in a slow troll will usually attract the flashy brookies. Fly anglers catch well during the first and last hours of daylight, especially in the shallower water.

Numerous small ponds and lakes lie scattered over the terrain around Irish and Taylor—both a blessing and a curse. Many of them hold fish, but they also serve as breeding grounds for mosquitoes, many of which find their way to Irish and Taylor early in the season. The largest of these outlying lakes, Brahma Lake, lies along the PCT about two miles north of Irish. Brook trout in this lake average 10 inches, but have been taken at 15 or better.

To reach Irish and Taylor Lakes from the west, take Highway 58 east from Oakridge to Forest Road 5897, signed to Waldo Lake. Continue north on this road to the North Waldo Lake campground, taking Forest Road 514 north toward Taylor Burn. After about 4½ miles, a signed junction leads right (east) about a mile to Irish and Taylor. This route is usually not accessible until late June. The road from the east opens around mid-June. (Check with the Bend Ranger District to be certain.) From Century Drive/Cascade Lakes Highway 46, take Forest Road 4630 west past Cultus Lake to the Little Cultus Lake

Taylor Lake

Road (No. 600). Follow this past Little Cultus Lake's south shore, about six miles to the lakes.

The roads from either direction (south or east) are unimproved, to say the least. Even in mid-July the Taylor Burn Road was pocked with puddles that could pass for lakes. It takes an ingenious wit to navigate all the obstacles, and a high-centered vehicle to clear the occasional rocky midcenter. Four-wheel-drive would be optimal, but old Blue Bart—our trusty '67 Ford Econoline van—made it through, albeit with shocks aged by several years. We would recommend a saw and a shovel as mandatory equipment (in case you get stuck).

The nearest supplies and gasoline are at the Cultus Lake Resort, about 12 miles to the east; Odell and Crescent Lake resorts to the southeast; and Oak-ridge, some 40 miles to the west.

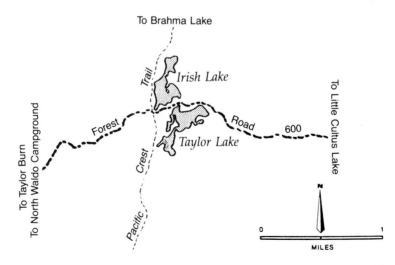

18
Link Creek Basin

Deschutes County
Deschutes National Forest
Distance from Corvallis: 89 miles

Link Lake dominates the group of small lakes in the Link Creek basin near Suttle Lake in the Deschutes National Forest, about 2½ miles south of the Santiam Highway (U.S. 20). From U.S. 20, drive four miles past the Hoodoo Ski Area turnoff to the Elliott R. Corbett III Memorial Snow Park (Forest Road 2076) and turn south. This gravel road takes you to Island, Link, Meadow, and Torso Lakes, among others. None of these small lakes receives heavy recreational use, so they're rather quiet despite their easy accessibility.

Along this road, you first encounter Island Lake, named for the rocky island at its center. The lake lies about two miles south of the highway and a short drive west into the lake on a signed dirt road. About 15 acres in size, it produces both rainbow and brook trout, averaging eight inches. There are no developed camp areas or boat ramps, but you'll find two natural sites for camping and can easily hand-launch your boat along the shore.

Next is Link Lake, about ¾ mile farther south, where fishing for cutthroat, rainbow, and brook trout can yield some fair-sized fish—up to 15 inches. Several natural campsites can be found, but no improvements.

Meadow and Torso lakes lie another mile south. Meadow Lake forms a bright spot in the center of a major burn area. A lightning-caused fire in 1967 burned the larger trees of the surrounding forest, but new growth is slowly softening the landscape, and Three Fingered Jack rises to the north. You have to walk a short distance down to the small lake because road access has been closed. About 16 acres, Meadow Lake holds rainbow, brook, and cutthroat trout. Early season brings the best fishing, just as soon as you can get in—usually in June—because the lake shrinks as the summer wears on.

Torso Lake, about half the size of Meadow, doesn't appear on the latest Forest Service map, but it rests sheltered in a hollow just to the east. Two nice but primitive campsites and access for launching a boat sit on the southwest shore. It's a more attractive setting than Meadow Lake, although one loses the view of Jack. The fishing doesn't compare with Meadow Lake, either, but Torso Lake does add the advantage of swimming in the heat of summer and tall firs that provide shade as well as cover for wildlife.

Two smaller lakes to the east along Forest Road 600, Cache and Hand Lakes, offer little recreational use because of the overgrowth of lily pads, but according to one source, Cache Lake does sport good-sized rainbow trout.

The nearest supplies are in Sisters, 26 miles to the east, or at the Clear Lake Resort, 18 miles southwest on Highway 126.

Island Lake

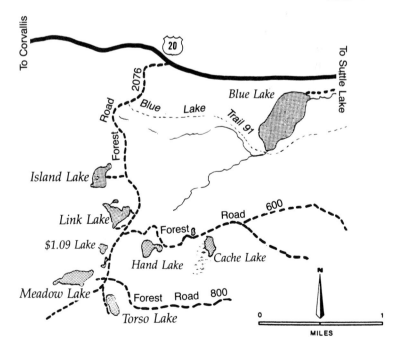

19
Linton Lake

Lane County
Willamette National Forest
Distance from Eugene: 73 miles

Countless motorists have probably driven through Deadhorse Grade in the McKenzie Pass with such intense concentration that they failed to notice the very small, somewhat obscured sign marking the trailhead into Linton Lake. We did—for years. We first noticed Linton Lake as a blue spot on the Willamette National Forest map, but even looking for it that small sign was hard to find. It took two passes along this serpentine stretch of highway for us to realize where the trail began.

With our eventual success, we discovered an easy 1½-mile trail that wound its way through volcanic outcroppings and coniferous forest down to a beautiful green lake nestled in a bowl-shaped canyon. The lava dam at the west end looks fresh, but it was formed some 3,000 years ago. The 50-acre lake created by the dam is quite deep (90 feet), and the steep slopes surrounding Linton provide shelter from high mountain winds.

As you near the lake on the trail, look to the southeast to catch a glimpse of Linton Falls, which you can hear roaring its welcome as you approach the lake. Take a good look, as this vantage point offers the only view of the falls. From the lake its presence is merely heard.

Many people come to Linton Lake simply for a day's fishing. The fishing is good, but the steep canyon limits space for camping, except for a few natural campsites on the east end. You have to travel carefully along the difficult, unmaintained user trail skirting three sides of the lake; in early season the trail can be muddy as well as steep.

Linton Lake lies within the Three Sisters Wilderness Area. Because of the relatively heavy use it receives, Linton has been the subject of Forest Service consideration for limiting "site impact," the alterations of natural processes and conditions caused by human activity. Therefore, it is imperative that visitors follow no-trace camping methods at Linton Lake.

For a sunny, open spot you can pitch your tent on the grassy, sandy point on the northeast shore. The most picturesque campsites lie to the southeast alongside Linton Creek, a cascading stream that plays a constant, rushing lullabye. A couple of large fallen trees form natural bridges across the creek.

If you don't want to pack in more than your fishing gear, you can camp at Alder Spring Campground, from which a trail leads directly to Linton, about 1½ miles.

Linton Lake

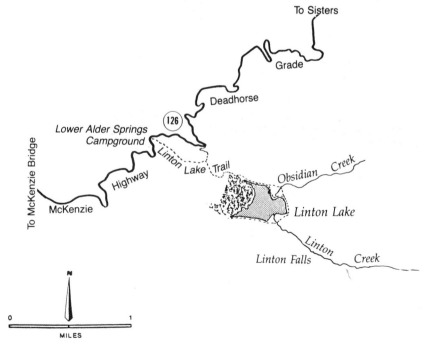

To Sisters

Grade

Deadhorse

126

Lower Alder Springs
Campground

To McKenzie Bridge

Linton Lake Trail

Highway

McKenzie

Obsidian Creek

Linton Lake

Linton Falls

Linton Creek

N

0   1

MILES

Although rarely what one might call "hot," fishing at Linton Lake is unique. It has the distinction of being the only high Cascade lake with a native population of German browns—the lunkers you see cruising through Linton's clear waters. Because of this special feature, many anglers practice catch-and-release fishing to preserve these large trout. Linton also supports native brook and rainbow trout, and rainbows are stocked regularly. All methods will catch fish, but several clear banks lend themselves well to fly casting. Your boat will be especially handy at Linton. The lake is small enough to maneuver around well in an inflatable raft, and the shore is not easily traversed—particularly the south shore and the lava dam at the west end. With a raft, you can fish this area, which holds some of the deepest water, without risking life and limb crossing the lava field.

When the fishing slows and the sun shines hot, take a plunge into the cool water for a bit of brisk refreshment. The lake floor drops off quickly, so swimming is not recommended for children without life gear. A shallower finger stretches west near where the trail touches the lake.

To reach the trailhead, take the McKenzie Pass Highway (242) about 15 miles east from McKenzie Bridge and 21 miles west of Sisters. You can park at Alder Spring Campground, where the 1½-mile trail takes off across the road. Sisters and McKenzie Bridge are the nearest sources of supplies.

Linton Creek

20
Lost Lake

Hood River County
Mt. Hood National Forest
Distance from Portland: 85 miles

Lost Lake, the setting for the cover photograph, is the archetypal Oregon lake: the pristine water, an incredible mountain view reflected in the glassy calm of the lake, the evergreen forest, a little mist rising in the dawn. So beautiful it doesn't quite seem real.

According to one account, Lost Lake was the setting of summer and autumn Indian gatherings and potlatches. One of 13 Lost Lakes in Oregon, this one was so christened because the 1880 scouting party trying to find it couldn't, at least initially. But, as with all 13, it, too, was eventually found.

Probably the largest lake in Oregon on which motors are prohibited, Lost Lake holds 231 acres and reaches a depth of 175 feet at its center.

Although heavily fished, the lake produces quite well through the early part of the season and then again around September. Because of the size of the lake, fish have room to grow—as the photographs in the resort store will evidence. German brown trout have been caught at over 12 pounds, rainbow (stocked annually) at a record 9½ pounds. Kokanee salmon can be caught through early summer, and brook trout are also found. Many of the regulars at Lost Lake prefer trolling slowly along the shoreline with small flatfish or flies.

Stop in at the resort's General Store for both tips and local tackle. The store stocks groceries and other supplies, and rents rowboats, paddle boats, and canoes, with life gear provided free. The store sells firewood, too, and you'll need it (or bring your own) if you're camping and want a campfire—anything there for foraging has long ago been used.

Seven modest cabins, sleeping two to 10 people, are available for rent. Guests must provide their own bedding and cooking utensils, but the cabins come equipped with kerosene lamps, wood stoves, rustic furniture, and water buckets with which to carry water from the faucets outside. Two cabins boast fireplaces. Hot showers can be enjoyed by resort patrons with tokens purchased in the General Store. Make your cabin reservations well in advance by writing to P. O. Box 1234, Estacada, OR 97023 (from September to May); during the season, write to P. O. Box 90, Hood River, OR 97031. The resort opens May 1; however, roads may not be accessible until later in the month. Call the Hood River Ranger District to be certain.

The fee campground at Lost Lake has more than 75 sites, all of which are often taken during peak summer weekends. (Early and late in season is the best time for solitude here.) Very few campsites rest right on the lake, but

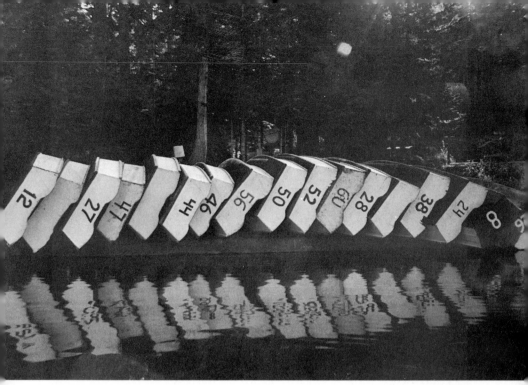

Lost Lake

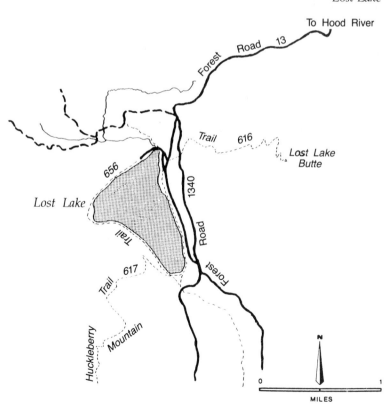

To Hood River

Forest Road 13

Trail 616

Lost Lake Butte

656

1340

Lost Lake

Trail 617

Forest Road

Huckleberry Mountain Trail

N

0   MILES   1

most offer at least a view. Many sites have a short but steep slope from the parking space to the tent site and table.

A hiking trail, No. 656, surrounds the lake, about three miles. At the north end of the lake near the Day Use Area you'll find a self-guided nature trail, the brochures for which can be purchased at the General Store. Other trails include the Huckleberry Mountain Trail (No. 617), which takes off from the southern tip of the lake and wanders 2½ miles through wild rhododendrons and huckleberries to connect with the Pacific Crest National Scenic Trail, and the Lost Lake Butte Trail (No. 616), which starts near the entrance to the campground and leads two miles to the butte. Lost Lake Butte, elevation 4,468 feet, affords a panoramic view of five Cascade peaks.

During the month of August the water has usually warmed enough to make the fish lethargic, so when they've stopped biting, it's time for swimming. The lake's size and depth, combined with a 3,000-foot elevation, means the water's never warm—it's what we hardy Oregonians call "refreshing."

To get to Lost Lake, take Interstate 84 east up the Columbia River Gorge to Hood River and State Highway 35, following signs southwest to Dee. From here the route to Lost Lake is well-signed. From Mt. Hood Highway 26, turn north from Zig Zag on Lolo Pass Road (Forest Road 18) and follow signs to Lost Lake. The route from Dee is usually open earlier—by mid-May or early June. You can check at the Zig Zag Ranger Station on Highway 26 to see whether the Lolo Pass road is open.

21
Lucky Lake

Deschutes County
Deschutes National Forest
Distance from Bend: 40 miles

The walk into Lucky Lake is an easy, gradual climb that'll take only about 30 minutes, so it makes a great day hike. But if you want to stay over, you'll find several natural campsites around the lake. South Sister rises to the north, adding to the quiet beauty of Lucky Lake. The water shines a rich turquoise that darkens to indigo in certain deep pools.

By midsummer, the rocky heat of Central Oregon might tempt you to shed your dusty garb and plunge into the water. A swim in Lucky Lake can be just the thing for a tired hiker when the fish aren't biting. There are even some nice sandy-bottomed spots along the shore. Bring your goggles—the water is nearly tropical in its color and clarity, if not its temperature.

If you like birds, you'll enjoy the close contact with them here. The gray jays are audacious connoisseurs of trail mix or any treats you might have. They're fun to attract, but be watchful—they'll snatch your lunch right out of your hand if you're not looking.

The fishing at Lucky Lake is fair to good for stocked cutthroat and brook trout, which range in size from eight to 16 inches. You can paddle around easily on Lucky's 30 acres in a rubber craft, and trolling with bait or spinners works better than bank fishing because of the submerged snags around the shore.

The lack of underbrush does make it possible to circle the lake by foot. The trail into the lake continues northwest to Senoj Lake, about four miles, then turns east to Blow and Doris Lakes (see separate entry). A trail leading southwest from Lucky takes you to the Corral Lakes (four miles) and Cultus Lake (seven miles).

To reach the Lucky Lake trailhead, drive southwest from Bend on the Cascade Lakes Highway 46 (Century Drive) about 40 miles, ¼ mile beyond the Lava Lake turnoff. The trail (No. 99) takes off from a parking area on the west side of the highway, leading 1¼ mile to the lake.

More developed camping can be had at Lava Lake or Little Lava Lake, only 1½ miles from the trailhead. Lava Lake also has a resort, where you can rent boats (for use on Lava Lake only) or purchase gas, groceries, and fishing tackle.

Lucky Lake

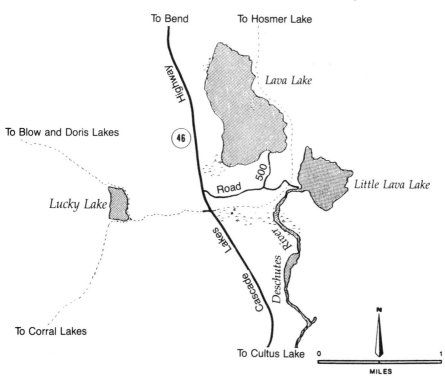

22
Marion Lake

Linn County
Willamette National Forest
Distance from Portland: 116 miles

Probably the best-known hike-in lake in the Cascades, Marion Lake is certainly the largest. At 360 acres, it surpasses all other hike-in lakes in the state. Named by John Minto's surveying party in the late 1800's for Revolutionary General Francis Marion, the lake lies in a deep glacial basin within the Mt. Jefferson Wilderness Area, a 2½-mile hike from the trailhead, which begins five miles from State Highway 22.

Three Fingered Jack raises its craggy peak above the southern horizon. The northeast shores offer both the best views and the best campsites. The Forest Service has begun restricting camping at Marion Lake because of the devastation caused by years of activity along its shoreline. Campsites must be well away from the shore, and no camping will be permitted where the trail comes into the lake. Check the notice board at the trailhead for areas newly specified as day-use only. Also, the use of any wheeled device to transport boats, supplies, or equipment into the lake has been prohibited. The Forest Service established these rules in 1986 to aid the restoration and maintenance of the area's wilderness character.

If you want a little seclusion, continue east beyond the large talus slope. Several little spur trails lead to more solitary campsites all along the way, and a couple of small streams provide both water and music. The point that juts into the middle of the lake is also a favorite.

The sites near the streams also have sandy-bottomed shallows with gradual slopes that make swimming safer for young campers. The water in these shallower areas warms nicely by late July or August. But stay clear of the stream path itself—that's cold mountain water flowing in.

You won't catch bucketsful of fish in Marion Lake, but you could catch some nice-sized ones, three to four pounds or better. The lake holds stocked rainbow trout and native brookies and cutts. Although it can be fished from shore, you'll appreciate your boat, both because of the size of the lake and because trolling bait, lures, or wet flies all find favor with the fish. The bite usually hits during early morning hours and around dusk.

Abundant wildlife around Marion includes deer, martin, and osprey, to name a few. You might also be welcomed by curious golden-mantle squirrels or a neighborly kangaroo mouse.

You can set out to explore some other lakes nearby, and be sure to take your fishing gear. You passed Ann Lake on the way in, about a mile back. This 16-

Marion Lake & Three Fingered Jack
Photograph courtesy of the Oregon Department of Tourism

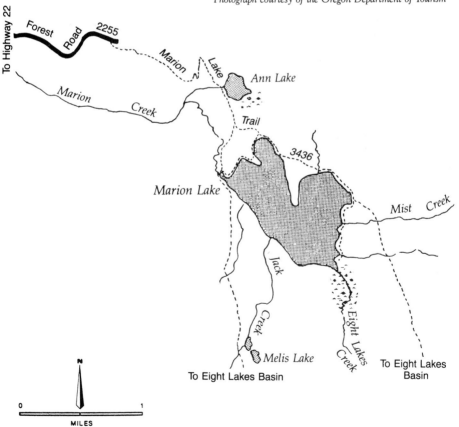

acre lake holds Eastern brook trout that grow to 15 inches and are especially fond of flies. The reeds surrounding Ann Lake make shore fishing difficult, so bring your inflatable along, too. The southwest shoreline and the area adjacent to the trail from the outlet to the rock slide have been designated as day use areas only.

Another trail south past Marion Lake takes you into the Eight Lakes Basin, about four miles. The trail loops back around the southern edge of Jorn Lake, and in six miles you're back at Marion. This would be an energetic loop to walk just for the day, but it's majestic country, laced with lakes and breathtaking scenery.

To reach the Marion Lake trailhead, take State Highway 22 southeast from Detroit about 16 miles to Forest Road 2255 at the Marion Forks Ranger Station. At the end of the road, about five miles, Trail No. 3436 begins its steady climb to the lake.

Marion Lake trout

23
Olallie Lakes National Scenic Area

Marion County
Mt. Hood National Forest
Distance from Portland: 80 miles

This spectacular 10,798-acre scenic area on the crest of the Cascade Range embraces some 30 lakes, with a dozen others just outside its boundaries. All are designated non-motorboat lakes, and they range in size from 238-acre Olallie Lake to three-acre First Lake.

The recreational experiences to be enjoyed at Olallie are nearly as various. Some 200 lakes and ponds lie scattered throughout the area around Olallie Butte. It would be easy to spend an entire month in the Olallie Lakes Scenic Area, exploring the various lakes, watching wildlife, boating and fishing. You can lodge overnight in a cozy cabin or pack your bedroll deep into the wilderness. From the docks at Olallie Lake you gaze directly on Mt. Jefferson's rugged north face. A rustic resort sells gas and groceries and offers boats and cabins for rent, and several lakes have developed campsites. You can hike in to any number of lakes for a wilderness adventure or climb to a 7,125-foot viewpoint atop the highest cinder cone in the Oregon Cascades.

This incredible basin of lakes derives its character from glacial activity during the Pleistocene Epoch. The name Olallie, applied to several geographic features in the state, comes from the Chinook word for berries, or huckleberries when used in the Cascade Range area. The Olallie Lake region sees a profusion of huckleberries, ripening by late August.

Olallie Lake

The largest lake in the region, Olallie Lake is extremely popular, and midsummer weekends will find nearly every campsite occupied. Midweek, however, and weekends in September's Indian summer of warm days and cool evenings still provide some solitude.

Olallie Lake has three developed areas: Paul Dennis on the northeast shore provides 15 sites plus three walk-in sites; Camp Ten is a popular campground but has only eight units; and Peninsula to the south is the largest, with 35 units plus three walk-ins and handicap facilities, including a fishing platform. Paul Dennis and Peninsula campgrounds require nightly fees, but both provide drinking water. All three campgrounds provide access to the Olallie Lake Trail (No. 731), which circles the lake (about three miles) and connects with trails to Monon Lake and to Long, Dark, Island, and Trout Lakes.

Olallie Lake & Mt. Jefferson

Fishing for rainbow, German brown, or brook trout can be excellent in Olallie and most of the area's lakes early in the season and in late September and into October. From Olallie's boat dock you can sometimes glimpse hulking brood trout cruising in the crystalline water below. You'll get lots of advice about current fishing activity from the resort store, but popular methods include trolling wet flies on a long, two-pound leader (the water is extremely clear, so lighter terminal tackle avoids spooking the fish) and trolling flatfish or flashers with bait (use three- to four-pound leader with the heavier tackle). Fish average 10 to 12 inches, with an occasional lunker over 20. Legal-size rainbows are stocked each season, along with a few brood trout.

Because Olallie serves as the water source for the area, the Forest Service discourages swimming. However, several smaller lakes nearby, such as First and Hand Lakes, are the perfect size and warm early.

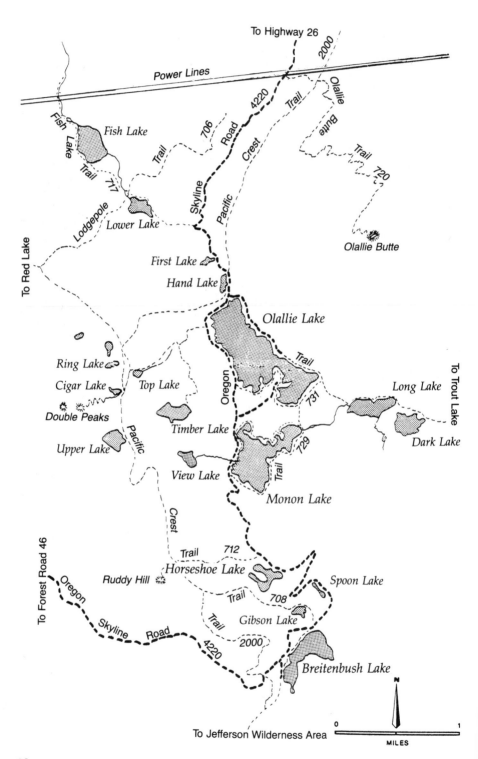

To Highway 26

Power Lines

2000

Olallie

4220

Crest

Trail

706

Road

Butte

Fish Lake

Fish Lake

Trail

Skyline

Pacific

Trail

720

Lower Lake

Lodgepole

Trail

717

Olallie Butte

To Red Lake

First Lake

Hand Lake

Olallie Lake

Ring Lake

Cigar Lake

Top Lake

Oregon

Trail

731

Long Lake

To Trout Lake

Double Peaks

Timber Lake

Pacific

729

Dark Lake

Upper Lake

View Lake

Trail

Monon Lake

Crest

To Forest Road 46

Trail

712

Horseshoe Lake

Ruddy Hill

Oregon

Trail

708

Spoon Lake

Skyline

Road

Trail

2000

Gibson Lake

4220

Breitenbush Lake

N

To Jefferson Wilderness Area

0   1

MILES

80

Monon Lake

Monon and Horseshoe Lakes

The nearest lake to the south, Monon Lake, measures 98 acres, the second-largest lake in the basin. Its clear waters offer good fishing for brook and rainbow trout, averaging around eight to 10 inches and running to 15. This lake receives much less activity, largely because of limited camping access. The road passes within a few yards of the shore on the west side, where a couple of tent spaces have been squeezed in between. But it's just a short walk on Trail No. 732 from Peninsula Campground to the northeast tip of Monon, so you could camp at Olallie and easily enjoy both lakes. The Monon Lake Trail (No.

729) circles the lake, which has several small bays worth exploring by boat as well.

About a mile south of Monon lies Horseshoe Lake. Although one might surmise that the lake was named for the two long arms that curve around a spit of land on the western shore, according to Lewis McArthur, author of *Oregon Geographic Names*, the lake received its name when someone found a horseshoe near its shore.

The clean white floor and clear water of shallow Horseshoe Lake give it a gem-like color. Its 15 acres also hold brook and rainbow trout, and although you'll enjoy floating around on this lake, a boat isn't a necessity for fishing.

By car, Horseshoe Lake lies three miles south of the Olallie Guard Station along a single-lane gravel road (Oregon Skyline Road 4220). Four walk-in campsites provide ample room for camping, but there is little space for parking.

About a half-mile south of Horseshoe Lake on the road to Breitenbush, a sharp switchback with a large gravel roadside marks the spot for a magnificent vista of the Olallie Area. Pull over and climb carefully to look over the rockpile alongside the road; the two large lakes you see are Monon and Olallie.

Two miles beyond, Breitenbush is the only other lake in the area to which one can drive, although many might argue that the road was not meant for vehicular travel (see Breitenbush Lake entry).

Hiking Trails and Lakes

As for hike-in lakes, take your pick. Probably the most popular is the 24-acre Fish Lake. The surrounding noble fir and mountain hemlock give it a beautiful setting for camping in the several natural spots on the northwest end of the lake. The lake's small brook and cutthroat trout are frequently sought after, but fishing can still be fair in early season and in late fall. Fish Lake reaches a depth of 67 feet, which suggests trolling with bait or lures as an effective fishing method. To reach the lake, take Fish Lake Trail No. 717 from Lower Lake Campground (¾ mile north of the Olallie Lake Guard Station off Skyline Road).

You'll hike one mile into Fish Lake, passing 16-acre Lower Lake about halfway in. If you decide not to pass it by, you'll find several suitable overnight spots and good fishing at Lower Lake for brook and rainbow trout. Despite its small size, Lower Lake reaches the greatest depth of any lake in the entire scenic area (73 feet).

Just north of Lower Lake, Lodgepole Trail No. 706 takes off to the west, leading to five smaller lakes. Red, Averill, Wall, Sheep, and Fork Lakes are relatively isolated and not as widely used as other lakes in the scenic area. All within 1½ miles of each other, they offer fair fishing (mostly for brook trout) throughout the season and several natural campsites at each.

Trails criss-cross the entire scenic area. A good map is usually available either at the resort store or the Guard Station at Olallie Lake. One other

Monon & Olallie Lakes

hike-in worth mentioning here lies at the end of the Timber Lake Trail No. 733. Timber Lake is another popular camping area in a peaceful setting of pacific silver fir, mountain hemlock, and huckleberries. Fishing for Eastern brook trout in the 10-acre lake runs fair throughout the season. Timber Lake can be reached via the Red Lake Trail (719) from Skyline Road about ¼ mile south of the Guard Station; hike west ¼ mile to the Timber Lake Trail and one mile south to the lake.

Other Area Lakes

Outside the scenic area's boundaries lie several small lakes, some within the Warm Springs Indian Reservation. Reservation permits are generally required for fishing; check with the Confederated Tribes of Warm Springs in Warm Springs (503) 553-1161.

To the southeast, these include Long, Dark, Island, and Trout Lakes, all fair-sized (about 16 acres) and accessible from the southeastern tip of Olallie Lake. From Paul Dennis Campground, walk south along Olallie's shore to the junction of Long Lake Trail (No. 730), which turns east about ¾ mile to the lake. Dark Lake, the deepest of these at 52 feet, lies about a mile beyond, following the north shore of Long Lake, and Trout Lake another 1½ miles. You'll pass Island Lake along the way.

To the north of Olallie Lake, about four miles from the Guard Station, you'll find Olallie Meadow Campground, a large, peaceful meadow with seven campsites. From here you can take the Russ Lake Trail (No. 716) about a mile into the five-acre brook trout lake. Along the way, you'll pass Brook Lake and, just off the trail on the PCT, Jude Lake. Not really a destination in themselves, these small lakes can be fun to explore on a day outing, and they'll provide a good day's fly fishing in autumn months, especially in the evening. Your boat will come in handy for fishing as the shorelines are surrounded by brush, which also makes camping difficult. Overnighters will want to stay at Olallie Meadow.

Getting There

The area is accessible usually by mid-June, but it's worth a call to check, as often one lingering snow drift can make the road impassable well into the month. (Our honeymoon in mid-June found us stuck in a snowdrift several miles from the main road. Fortunately a Forest Ranger followed us in and helped dig us out.) Contact the Clackamas Ranger District for current information.

The best map for finding Olallie is the Mt. Hood National Forest Map. The scenic area lies in the southeastern corner of the forest. To get to Olallie Lake via State Highway 26, take Forest Road 42 south. Follow route 42 to Warm Springs Meadow and turn south on Forest Road 4220 (Oregon Skyline Road), a single-lane dirt and gravel road, following signs to Olallie. The distance

Brook Lake

from Highway 26 is approximately 35 miles.

From the west, Olallie can be reached via State Highway 22. At Detroit, turn northeast on Forest Road 46 (Breitenbush River Road), continuing east past the Breitenbush Campground. Just beyond the powerline crossing, take Forest Road 4220 east. This road is shorter but a great deal rougher than the northern route for the first seven to eight miles. You'll pass Breitenbush, Horseshoe, and Monon Lakes via this route to Olallie.

24
Opal & Timpanogas Lakes

Douglas County
Willamette National Forest
Distance from Eugene: 90 miles

Set in glacial basins along the Cascade Divide, stands of tall Pacific silver, mountain hemlock, and noble fir enclose these high-mountain lakes at the far southeastern edge of the Willamette National Forest. Only a few miles south of popular Summit Lake, both Opal and Timpanogas are great for getting away from the crowds. They receive only light to moderate use because of the short season and the active mosquitoes. Although the lakes are accessible in mid-June, according to the Forest Service most visitors wait until August to avoid the skeeters.

Opal Lake, the smaller of the two, has only one tent site with table. The single-lane gravel road passes about two-tenths of a mile from the lake, so camping gear and boats must be carried in. Brook trout in Opal Lake average 10 inches. Anglers most commonly use bait, although lures will also attract a few nibbles.

Timpanogas Lake at 40 acres measures about three times the size of Opal and is proportionately more popular. The small campground, located around the west to south shores, has facilities that include tables, fire rings, and one hand pump for well water. Canoes and other boats can be launched at your campsite, but there is no boat ramp.

At Timpanogas, brook and cutthroat trout average about 10 inches and can best be lured to your line by slow-trolling along the northwest shore.

A walking trail loops around the lake's edge, crossing a steep talus slope to the east. A two-mile trail takes off from the campground and climbs to 20-acre Indigo Lake. Sawtooth Mountain dominates the skyline at Indigo, which lies at about 6,000-foot elevation. Indigo once harbored a developed camp area, and though it is no longer maintained, the campsite does have picnic tables and a rustic privy.

June Lake lies southwest of Timpanogas about 2½ miles. A three-mile trail climbs from the campground up to 10-acre June Lake, which holds brook trout and is only lightly fished. The limited camping area makes June Lake best for day trips from one of the larger lakes.

To reach Opal Lake, take Highway 58 from Oakridge to Forest Road 21, which turns south and follows the shore of Hills Creek Lake. After about 33 miles, turn left on Forest Road 2154, which turns to gravel after about four miles. Follow Forest Road 2154 to Opal Lake (about ¼ mile); turn south on Forest Road 399 to Timpanogas Lake (about ½ mile). The nearest gas and supplies are in Oakridge, about 45 miles.

Photograph courtesy of the Oregon Department of Fish & Wildlife   *Opal Lake*

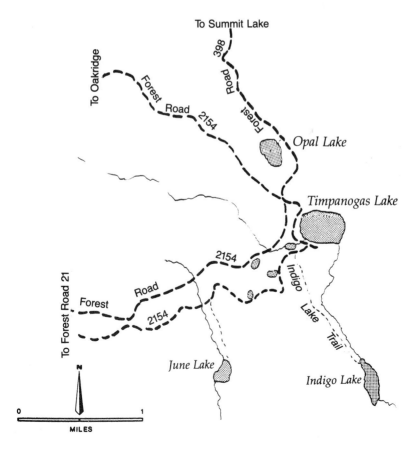

25
Pamelia Lake

Linn County
Willamette National Forest
Distance from Portland: 113 miles

Settled at the foot of Mt. Jefferson, Pamelia Lake gives one the impression of being on a lake in the Alps. It lies in a deep valley at the base of Oregon's second tallest mountain, and the scenery takes your breath away. Not surprisingly, it's one of the favorite hike-in lakes in the state, and because it rests within the Jefferson Wilderness Area, visitors must take special care to preserve Pamelia Lake's natural environment.

The aesthetic enjoyment of Pamelia begins long before you reach the lake. The easy trail follows cascading Pamelia Creek through a lush forest. Carved by glaciers in ages long gone by, Pamelia Lake holds nearly 45 acres in a shallow basin, a surprising 15-foot depth considering the steep slopes that rise above the shoreline.

The lake and its outlet stream were named for Pamelia Ann Berry, a young girl who served as cook for the John Minto scouting party in the 1870's and who "always exhibited unfailing cheerfulness." But in the midst of this beautiful setting, who wouldn't be cheerful?

Primitive campsites at Pamelia Lake are plentiful, beginning at the point where the trail meets the lake and all along the northeastern shore, with several others along the lake's primary tributary, Hunts Creek. The sites farther in offer the most privacy, as the trail comes close to or through the more westerly camps. Also toward the northeast several smaller unnamed tributaries rush into the lake, providing an excellent water source. The glacial water from these streams runs extremely cold and clear and has that sweetness characteristic of high mountain springs. (As always, water should be treated before drinking.)

The lake fairly bursts with small cutthroat trout—and the little fellas will jump at just about anything. The 30-fish-per-day limit is an attempt to control the overpopulation, cutting down on the competition for available food and allowing more room for the fish to grow to greater sizes. Fish currently average four to eight inches, and your boat will be useful for fishing. Although a fishing trail circles the lake, the brushy north shore and steep south shore make walking around the lake difficult. As the water line recedes later in summer, the shore can be walked more easily.

But the real lure of this lake lies in its serene, alpine setting. It's a great place to spend a couple of lazy days just drifting with the cool mountain breeze. The days at Pamelia Lake run longer than one might expect because of the contour of the valley. The sun sets through the deep V at the western

Pamelia Lake & Mt. Jefferson

edge of the lake, casting lingering rays well beyond the usual hour for dusk in the mountains. In August, look for a profusion of butterflies fanning their bright blue wings along the shore.

Swimming is cool but refreshing in later summer months. Take along some old tennis shoes for wading on the sharp, rocky bottom.

Some backpackers set up base camp at Pamelia for hikes farther into the Jefferson Wilderness Area. The trail along the northeast shore follows sparkling Hunts Creek about four miles to Hunts and Hanks Lakes, which command amazing views of Mt. Jefferson and Cathedral Rocks. The lush meadow areas are ablaze with wildflowers in July.

From State Highway 22, about seven miles south of Idanha, turn east on Pamelia Creek Road (Forest Road 2246) and drive about four miles to the Pamelia Lake Trail (No. 3439). There's a garbage container and an outhouse at the trailhead. The easy trail follows Pamelia Creek for 2¼ miles to the lake.

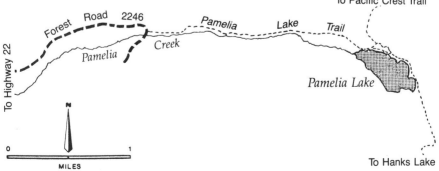

89

26
Roslyn Lake

Clackamas County
Distance from Portland: 30 miles

The only lake in *Quiet Waters* that lies on private land, owned and maintained by Portland General Electric, Roslyn Lake hums with activity on hot summer weekends when Portlanders escape the rigors of city life in exchange for a close-in day of paddling. If you live in the Portland area and just have a day to get away, Roslyn Lake is perfectly situated for hop-in-the-car spontaneity. Only 45 minutes from the city, Roslyn Lake offers opportunities for year-round boating and fishing.

Roslyn Lake Park, on the south shore, opens for day use only from 8 a.m. to 8 p.m. daily during summer months. On summer weekends, expect to pay a nominal fee to enter the park. Facilities include picnic tables, grills, horseshoe pits, and playfields for games of softball or volleyball (bring your own equipment). Large groups may reserve sheltered areas complete with barbecue pits, electric stoves, and running water.

A concessionaire sells snacks and drinks, and you can rent canoes, rowboats, or paddle boats at the lake.

Fishing can be good in spring and late fall for stocked rainbow trout. Occasionally brood trout are released into the lake, which accounts for the reports of giants caught at Roslyn.

Hot days find people taking to the water for a cooling swim, but more in the early summer before the algae takes hold. The lake shore slopes gradually, making it ideal for children.

To get to Roslyn Lake, take U.S. Highway 26 east from Portland. Just east of Sandy, turn north onto Ten Eyck Road and follow signs to Roslyn Lake, about 3½ miles north of U.S. 26.

Photograph courtesy of Portland General Electric

Roslyn Lake

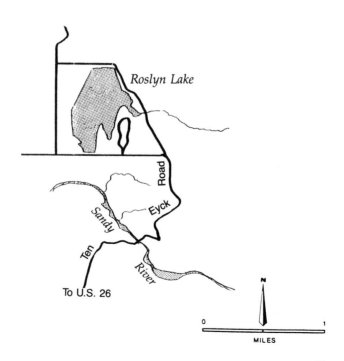

Roslyn Lake

To U.S. 26

MILES

27
Round Lake

Jefferson County
Deschutes National Forest
Distance from Sisters: 20 miles

High in the Cascades, Round Lake can be far from quiet. It plays host each summer to several church groups, and the peace is sometimes shattered by kids trying to drench one another in raucous water fights.

But all this good fun aside, Round Lake does offer some weeks of solitude in May and September and the odd week during the summer. If you have children, the profusion of young campers may be an advantage. But if you want to avoid the extra noise and confusion, you can check with the Sisters Ranger District to see whether the camp is being rented.

A small developed campground at Round Lake provides picnic tables and fire pits. A couple of sites adjacent to the outlet stream are especially nice. On a lazy afternoon, take a book over to the stream, prop yourself against a fallen log, and enjoy a long nap in the sun.

As far as mountain lakes go, Round Lake is ideal for swimming, often as early as late June. You'll even find a log raft often used for sunbathing mid-lake.

The osprey hovering overhead indicate that fish can be found in the lake. In fact, when swimmers aren't sending the fish to the bottom, fishing runs fair to good here, especially early and late in the season. Brook and rainbow trout are stocked annually, and fish caught average about 10 inches, though a few over 16 inches have been taken.

You can explore the lake on foot, too. A path follows the lake shore, and a leisurely stroll takes about 30 minutes. If you'd like more seclusion than Round Lake sometimes offers, try the short hike up to Long Lake. The trailhead begins about ½ mile beyond the campground (park about 200 yards from the Round Lake Christian Camp) and leads west to Long Lake (about a mile and a half) and on to Square Lake (another ½ mile). From there, other trails will take you north into the Eight Lakes Basin.

The trail to Long Lake climbs a steep grade, especially at first, and the lake can be hard to spot from the trail. One clue: when you pass through the boggy meadow, keep your eyes open for spur trails leading off to the left. Hidden from view, the lake lies about 100 yards from the Square Lake Trail. Once there, you'll find several natural campsites on the south shore. This long and narrow lake also offers fair fishing for small brook and cutthroat trout throughout the season. Come prepared for mosquitoes, as the lake borders a large and

Round Lake

sometimes marshy meadow. For a description of Square Lake, see the separate entry.

To get to Round Lake, take U.S. Highway 20 east from its junction with State Highway 22. About ½ mile beyond the Suttle Lake turnoff, turn north on Forest Road 12 (Jack Creek Road), then west on Forest Road 1210 to the campground. Road 1210 makes a full circle; the southern route turns west about a mile north of U.S. 20, but the northern route (two miles from U.S. 20) is the best road.

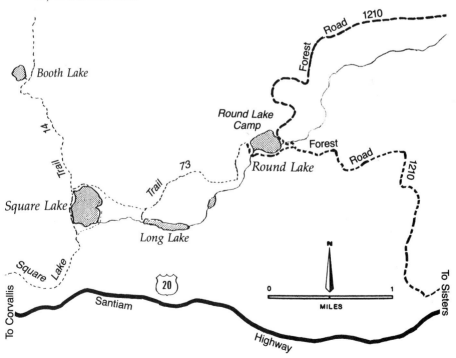

28
Scott Lake

Lane County
Willamette National Forest
Distance from Eugene: 74 miles

This enchanting lake in the McKenzie Pass area affords a dramatic view of South and Middle Sisters, often mirrored in the still waters of Scott Lake. Named for Felix Scott, an early promoter of the McKenzie toll road, the lake covers some 26 very shallow acres and actually consists of several pools strung together by a series of narrow channels. The first of these channels dries up over the summer, but it's an easy portage to cross over into the next pool.

Canoeists especially enjoy Scott Lake because it's so interesting to explore, and because the pristine setting is not easily rivaled. A developed campsite rests on the western shore of the lower pools, but peak summer weekends often find these spots filled. Those interested in solitude often boat or walk in to natural sites to be found along other shores. The lake provides the only source of water, so come prepared to treat it for drinking.

Scott does not produce much fishing activity, but it offers several other attractions in addition to its beauty. Your children will enjoy the tiny frogs that populate the marshy banks of Scott Lake in August. The water gets warm early, often by mid-July, and swimming from your boat can be fun, especially in the deeper sections of the larger pools. (The fine layers of pumice on the bottom stir easily, and swimming from shore requires walking out through several inches of sediment.)

Those interested in fishing might try a walk into Benson Lake, 1½ miles northwest of the campground. Benson sports a natural population of brookies that average eight to 10 inches. About a mile to the north of Benson, the three small Tenas Lakes offer fishing for brook, cutthroat, and rainbow. If it's hiking you're after, stay on the trail and it will lead you to viewpoints atop Scott Mountain, elevation 6,116 feet. Another trail from the campground takes off to the northeast of Scott Lake, leading to Hand Lake, which lies just inside the Mt. Washington Wilderness Area.

To get to Scott Lake Campground, take the McKenzie Highway 242 west from Sisters about 23 miles to Forest Road 1532 (one mile north of Frog Campground) and turn west about a mile. The nearest supplies are in Sisters. Another nearby attraction is the Dee Wright Observatory above the massive lava fields of the Mt. Washington Wilderness Area, about five miles east at McKenzie Pass.

Scott Lake & Sisters

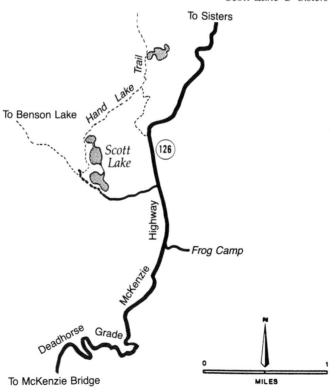

29
Sparks Lake

Deschutes County
Deschutes National Forest
Distance from Bend: 26 miles

Sparks Lake is just too captivating, too special, to be omitted from a book on quiet waters of Oregon, even though motorboats are allowed. Dominated by a spectacular view of South Sister, Sparks combines picture-postcard beauty with a bounty of recreational opportunities.

The few motorboats used here do little to mar the serenity of the lake. The speed limit in force is 10 miles per hour, and motors cannot be running while fishing. Also, the lake is so shallow—only two feet average—that motors can easily get stuck in the volcanic mud at the bottom, so not a lot of motorboats are to be found.

Canoeists love Sparks Lake because of the several shallow inlets that stretch into the craggy outcroppings of volcanic rock bordering the southern pool of the lake. Paddling silently, you can explore these fingers, or the shallow marsh area of the north end, sometimes surprising a family of deer. In fact, there's a great deal of wildlife to be observed at Sparks: several species of ducks, osprey, egrets, deer, and elk.

Altogether, the lake covers nearly 600 acres. Limited to fly fishing only, Sparks Lake provides a habitat for stocked rainbow and Eastern brook trout that can run to 16 inches or better, although they average closer to 10.

The deeper southern pools generally offer the best fishing, especially for drifting a wet fly. The shallow shoals of the northern portion are good for dry casting.

The extreme northern pool lies apart from the larger body of the lake, separated by a marshy meadow and connected by a small stream. It would be rare to find a motorboat on this section because the extremely shallow water makes access difficult, even for canoes. Earlier in the season, the tributary stream flows high enough into this part of the lake that you can put in at the small campsite at the end of an unmarked gravel road, about a mile west of the Sparks Lake turnoff and 1½ miles east of Devils Lake.

From here you can sometimes paddle in early season into the main lake along a shallow stream through the marsh that separates the two pools. The stream flows from the southwest corner of the smaller section.

A standard boat ramp at the end of the spur road signed to Sparks Lake makes the main lake much more accessible. The campground lies just off the highway, about a mile from the lake, adjacent to Soda Creek. However, sev-

Sparks Lake

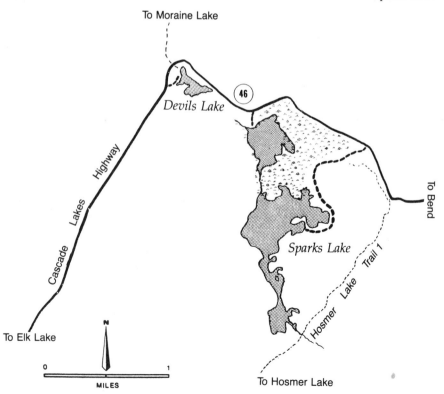

To Moraine Lake

Devils Lake

46

Cascade Lakes Highway

To Elk Lake

N

0   1

MILES

To Bend

Sparks Lake

Hosmer Lake Trail 1

To Hosmer Lake

eral pull-off-the-road sites exist nearer the boat ramp. None of the campsites are well designated, and you'll find few improvements besides outhouses.

Perhaps the best camping can be found by boat at the south end of the lake. It requires that your gear be portable, and that you arrive with enough daylight left to find your way.

Swimming at Sparks can be enjoyable once the water has warmed, but only the southern waters provide enough depth to get more than your knees wet. Beware of large boulders under water—diving is not recommended.

At the southern tip of the lake, the Hosmer Lake Trail passes one of the small fingers of Sparks, leading about three miles to Hosmer (see separate entry for description).

Passable by mid-June, the road to Sparks Lake turns south off Century Drive (Cascade Lakes Highway 46) 26 miles west of Bend, about four miles west of the Mt. Bachelor Ski Area. Soda Creek Campground is just off the highway on this road; the boat ramp and lake are at its end. One mile beyond this turnoff, a primitive road (with no markings besides the number 426) turns south ¼ mile to a small campsite. Neither the road nor the campsite appears on the Deschutes National Forest map.

The nearest supplies are at Elk Lake Resort, about seven miles southwest along Century Drive, where you can purchase gasoline, groceries, fishing tackle, and other supplies. The resort also operates a restaurant and rents cabins.

30
Square Lake

Deschutes County
Deschutes National Forest
Distance from Corvallis: 87 miles

Three Fingered Jack overlooks this hike-in lake at the crest of the Santiam Pass in the Cascades. Often hiked past by backcountry enthusiasts on their way to the Eight Lakes Basin, Square Lake offers a solitary wilderness experience without an arduous trek.

You'll find several ideal campsites along the east and southwest shores of the lake, all with views of the craggy Jack. Our favorite spot sits atop a small, rocky point that stretches out into the lake from the east shore. Three curious deer—the local version of the "Welcome Wagon"—stopped by for a brief visit in the early evening.

The campsites along the southern shore rest near sandy beaches, where the lake floor deepens gradually—great for youngsters who'd like to swim. The water usually warms enough for most folks by mid-July.

As with most of Oregon's quiet lakes, beauty and serenity rest easily on Square Lake. Take the time to walk around the lake—you cover quite a range of topography and flora. On the southwestern shore a glistening stand of silver firs shows dramatically against the rust-red of the forest floor. On the north an alpine meadow comes alive with wildflowers during early summer.

The osprey working this lake attest to the presence of fish—stocked brook and cutthroat average around nine to 10 inches. Although the lake is heavily fished, trolling slowly with wet flies, bait, or lures will usually work. The deeper waters on the north side of the lake offer fair bank fishing, with the bite coming on in the early morning and evening hours. Because Square Lake sits so near the crest of the mountain range, it nearly always has a breeze breaking the water's surface—good news for fly anglers.

Another good fishing lake lies just east about a mile along the outlet creek. For information about Long Lake, see the Round Lake entry.

Trail No. 65 continues north of Square Lake to Booth Lake, a small, eight-acre lake on the slopes of Three Fingered Jack that sustains brook and rainbow trout. It's about 1½ miles.

To reach the Square Lake trailhead, take U.S. Highway 20 through the Santiam Pass. Directly north across the road from the Hoodoo Ski Area, signs point to a large parking area for the Pacific Crest National Scenic Trail. Follow the PCT north about ¼ mile to the junction with Trail No. 65, which turns east 1½ miles to Square Lake. You can also hike into Square Lake via

Square Lake

Round and Long Lakes. See Round Lake for directions. The lake is usually accessible in June; contact the Sisters Ranger District to be sure.

The nearest supplies are at either Blue Lake Resort (roughly 10 miles) or Sisters (22 miles).

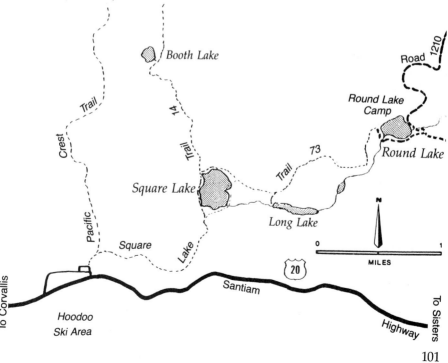

31
Squaw Lakes

Jackson County
Rogue River National Forest
Distance from Medford: 32 miles

Enlightened southern Oregonians have been traveling to these peaceful lakes in a basin of well-forested hills near the California border for years. Recently, the Forest Service has limited recreational use to preserve the lake's shoreline, but even so the use continues to be light to moderate throughout the summer. Holiday weekends, however, book up quickly.

Campers must make reservations in advance, for a small fee, and may only camp at the larger of the two Squaw Lakes. Drinking water in summer pours from two hand pumps; during the remainder of the year, bring your own or use the lake (treated, of course). The campsites line the lake's edge, beginning ¼ mile from the parking area. Facilities include tables and fire pits with cooking grills.

Open year-round for fishing, Squaw Lakes sustain stocked rainbow and cutthroat as well as catfish and crappie. Most anglers at these lakes prefer bait fishing.

If you walk the trail that circles the big lake, keep your eyes and ears peeled for rattlesnakes. They're not plentiful, but they have been seen in this area. A snake-bite kit would be a wise addition to your camping gear. Other wildlife to be on the lookout for are deer and a very occasional bear. The most prevalent species, however, are the cows that wander to the lakes from neighboring cattle ranches.

Little Squaw Lake lies about ½ mile southeast of the large lake along Forest Road 1075. The smaller lake offers picnicking and good fishing, but no camping. Both lakes warm enough for swimming, usually by mid-July.

The nearest gasoline and supplies are about 13 miles northwest of the lakes at the Upper Applegate Store—combination gas station, restaurant, tavern, grocery store, post office—near McKee Bridge, an historic covered bridge over the Applegate River.

To get to Squaw Lakes from Interstate 5, take State Highway 238 from Medford through Jacksonville to Ruch, in all about 13 miles. Turn south on the Upper Applegate Road to Applegate Reservoir (13 miles) and cross the dam to Forest Road 490, which follows Squaw Creek another six miles to the lakes.

Photograph courtesy of Portland State University, Geography Dept.   *Squaw Lake*

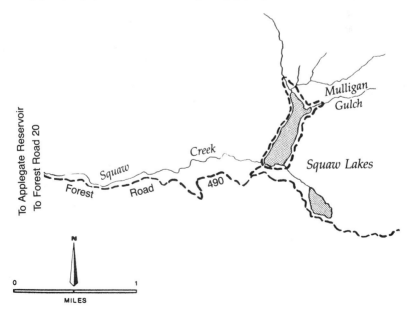

103

32
Summit Lake

Clackamas County
Mount Hood National Forest
Distance from Portland: 86 miles

Situated between Trillium Lake and the Olallie Lakes Scenic Area, Summit Lake lies just a mile off the highway. But the primitive road leading to this tiny lake deters a lot of traffic, often leaving the ducks on the lake as your only companions. Its rush-lined shores adjoin a forest of pine and hemlock, and some Forest Service improvements to the camp area make for comfortable overnight stays. We often stop over here for a quiet float on our way to other lakes in the area.

A sunny lake, it's nice just to float around in midday, soaking up the serenity, reading a good book, or taking a dip in the warm water. Although June will often find patches of snow left about, the fairly shallow lake usually warms by July. Swimmers will probably do best to find a deeper spot and then swim from the boat as the lake's silty floor stirs easily, making the water appear muddy.

You'll find a few creature comforts at the small campground, including a couple of nice campsites near the lake's edge, complete with fire places and picnic tables. There are outhouses, but no drinking water.

To get there take U. S. Highway 26 south from its junction with State Highway 35 and then turn southwest on Forest Road 42. Continue about five miles south of Clackamas Lake to a signed spur road (No. 141) and turn west (right) one mile to Summit Lake. The road climbs steeply at first and is not maintained, but it's short enough that most vehicles can make it.

Summit Lake

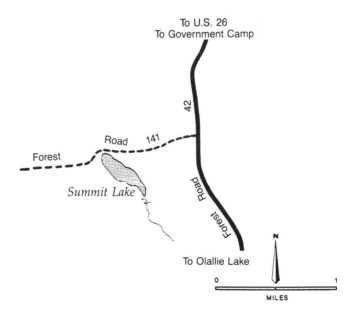

To U.S. 26
To Government Camp

42

Forest Road 141

Forest

Summit Lake

Road

Forest

To Olallie Lake

N

0   1

MILES

33
Three Creeks Lake

Deschutes County
Deschutes National Forest
Distance from Bend: 39 miles

Just 17 miles south of Sisters, Three Creeks Lake has for years been a favorite for families because it offers a lot to explore with children. The two campgrounds provide sandy beaches for playing and wading along shore, and an easy trail follows a small brook up to Little Three Creeks Lake.

Three Creeks Lake maintains a pristine quality despite several developments around its shores. The lake reaches a 30-foot maximum depth, but its dark blue color makes it seem even deeper. The water is so clear, though, that you can see the bottom even at its deepest point.

The name Three Creeks (sometimes Three Creek) comes from the joining of the three outfall streams of both lakes and Snow Creek Ditch, which come together to become Three Creeks, a stream that eventually flows into Squaw Creek.

To accommodate all the visitors, Three Creeks has two good-sized campgrounds at the lake, and another a mile before you reach the lake at Three Creeks Meadow, generally used by horse campers. At the lake, you first come to Driftwood Campground on the north shore, and Three Creeks Campground lies about ¼ mile beyond. A small store between the two carries groceries and some fishing tackle as well as row boats for rent by the day or by the hour.

Although campgrounds generally fill to capacity on peak weekends, during the week it's fairly quiet. And if you're prepared to carry your gear, you can always walk the mile up to Little Three Creeks Lake and camp there, without the usual campground amenities. The signed trail to Little Three Creeks follows the creek west from Driftwood Campground.

This stream once flowed directly into Three Creeks Meadow but has since been diverted through Three Creeks Lake. It's a pretty little brook, running around grassy knolls and through lodgepole pine forest. Children will enjoy searching for fingerling brook trout in the creek.

Whether you camp at the little lake or not, the easy trail makes it great for a day trip. The meadow full of wildflowers and the beautiful mountain views alone are worth the walk, but if you carry along your rod and reel, you'll find excellent fly angling for Eastern brookies as well. If the timing's right, kids will flip over meadow, which literally jumps with tiny frogs in late summer.

Three Creeks Lake

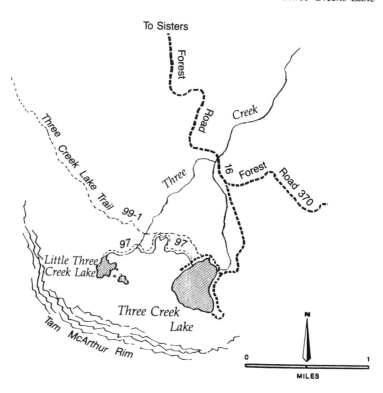

Adventuresome hikers might want to take the 2½-mile trek up to the 1,000-foot-high summit of Tam McArthur Rim, the glacially carved rock wall that rises dramatically above the big lake. Named for the original author of *Oregon Geographic Names*, the rim commands spectacular views of the snow-covered Cascade peaks. Trail No. 88 takes off opposite the entrance to Driftwood Campground.

Anglers give Three Creeks a good rating for stocked rainbow and natural brook trout. The proprietors of the store can proffer advice on what the fish are taking, but usually just about any method will yield a catch if you're persistent. The fish average around 10 inches, but both brookies and rainbow can run to 15.

By late July or August the water beckons you for a swim, and both campgrounds have some nice sandy beach areas with gradual dropoffs. A few windsurfers have strutted their stuff on the 75-acre lake. The winds blow strong enough but not too strong, making it a good place to learn. (Bend is the nearest source of rentals.)

To reach Three Creeks Lake, take Elm Street (which soon becomes Forest Road 16) south from Sisters about 17 miles. The road is paved except for the last ½ mile into the lake. Sisters is the nearest source of gasoline, but supplies can be purchased at the lake store. At nearly 6,500-foot elevation, the lake is usually accessible by mid-June, although an occasional snowdrift can keep the road closed into July. Check with the Sisters Ranger District to be sure.

Three Creeks Lake Store

34
Todd Lake

Deschutes County
Deschutes National Forest
Distance from Bend: 25 miles

If it were possible to rate Oregon's quiet lakes by virtue of their beauty alone, Todd Lake would certainly fall near the top of the list. Pristine in every regard, Todd Lake captures a sense of wilderness just a few hundred yards from the road. A friend said it best as she sat in the green meadow gazing on snow-capped Mt. Bachelor: "What did we do to deserve this?"

Though arguably we don't deserve it, we can enjoy so much at Todd Lake—most especially the scenery. The lake lies in a broad valley carved by glaciers, and the Three Sisters rise majestically to the northwest, with Mt. Bachelor guarding the southern horizon. A wide, grassy meadow blooms with wildflowers in late summer, and the glassy calm of the lake at dusk quiets the soul.

Once among the many "Lost Lakes" in Oregon, Todd acquired its name when Bend citizens chose to commemorate "Uncle" John Young Todd, an early settler in central Oregon.

Fishing in Todd Lake peaks shortly after ice-out, when you can first get to the lake (usually mid-June), but it tapers off quickly as the summer progresses. The Eastern brook trout can reach 15 inches, and they're especially fond of flies. A trail circles the lake, making it easy to fish from nearly any bank. The deeper southern portion of the lake reaches a maximum depth of 60 feet. The northern portion is about 20 feet deep. Fishing is prohibited from any floating craft, but just paddling around on Todd Lake fills an afternoon beautifully.

Youngsters enjoy playing in the sand and slow trickle of the small outlet stream at the southern edge of the lake. The lake here drops off gradually, but the floor on the western and eastern shores slopes more steeply.

A small, semi-developed campground sits just a hundred yards from the road. The improvements include outhouses and a few picnic tables and fire rings, but no drinking water. Road access to the lake has been closed to motor vehicles, so you have to walk your boat and gear the short distance to the camp area.

To get to Todd Lake, take Century Drive (Cascade Lakes Highway 46) southwest from Bend about 25 miles. Two miles west of the Mt. Bachelor Ski Area, turn north on a signed gravel road, about ¼ mile to the parking area and lake trail. The lake sits at 6,150 elevation and is usually accessible by mid to late June; check with the Bend Ranger District office.

The nearest supplies are at Elk Lake Resort, about 10 miles southwest on Century Drive, where you can purchase gasoline, groceries, fishing tackle, and other supplies, or dine in the restaurant or stay overnight in a rustic cabin.

Todd Lake & Broken Top

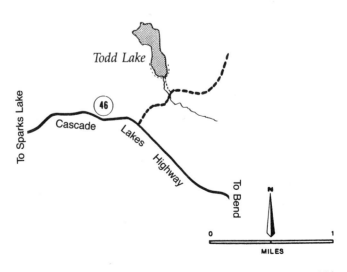

35
Torrey & Wahanna Lakes

Lane County
Willamette National Forest
Distance from Eugene: 71 miles

Hundreds of small lakes and ponds dot the newly designated, 37,000-acre Waldo Lake Wilderness Area. Torrey and Wahanna Lakes, at 70 and 60 acres in size, measure larger than average for the area, and they lie just a little more than a mile off the road.

Set in a dense forest of mountain hemlock and lodgepole pine, Torrey and Wahanna offer uncommonly good fishing for Eastern brook, cutthroat, and rainbow (rainbow only at Wahanna). Every couple of years, fingerling trout are stocked by air and left to grow to legal size. The shallow lakes are rich in nutrients, so fish grow rapidly, averaging 10 to 14 inches and better. Most anglers pack in a rubber raft for trolling ford fenders or spoons with bait. In the fall, fly fishing can be exceptional.

As a wilderness area, no camping improvements exist within its boundaries. You will find several natural sites around the lakes, but "without a trace" camping etiquette is de rigueur. Or you could camp at North Waldo and use daytime hours to explore these backcountry lakes.

As the summer wears on and warms these mountain lakes, swimming can be a great way to wile away the afternoon. Both lakes offer some nice shore areas.

You can easily spend several days poking about the lakes in this region. From the west end of Torrey Lake, a spur trail leads about 200 yards to narrow, 15-acre Whig Lake, an especially good fly lake that yields brookies to 16 inches. From Wahanna Lake, Trail No. 3583 leads south to Harvey and Kiwa Lakes, then cuts southeast to Rigdon Lakes, joining Trail No. 3590, which circles Waldo Lake. In all, it's about 4½ miles from Wahanna to North Waldo Campground.

To the north, Trail No. 3583 takes off toward Taylor Burn Guard Station, passing tiny Emma Lake along the way. Just beyond the station, the three Erma Bell Lakes also offer excellent fishing. From Wahanna, it's about 1½ miles to Taylor Burn, another 1½ to Upper Erma Bell.

To reach the trailhead into Torrey and Wahanna Lakes, drive east from Oakridge on State Highway 58 about 23 miles to the Waldo Lake Road (Forest Road 5897) and turn north. Follow signs to North Waldo Campground, 13 miles, and turn north on Taylor Burn Road, No. 514. This single-lane dirt and gravel road can present some obstacles that require tricky navigation, especially early in the season. But you only have to travel 2½ miles to the

Photograph reprinted with permission from Atlas of Oregon Lakes   *Torrey Lake*

trailhead, on the west side of the road. The Whig-Torrey Way Trail does not appear on the latest Forest Service map, but you shouldn't have trouble spotting the small parking area at the trailhead. The walk into Torrey is about 1¼ miles; Wahanna lies to the southwest about ½ mile beyond.

The longer trail (No. 3583) that appears on the Forest Service map comes into these lakes from the Taylor Burn area, but the road to that trailhead requires a four-wheel-drive vehicle.

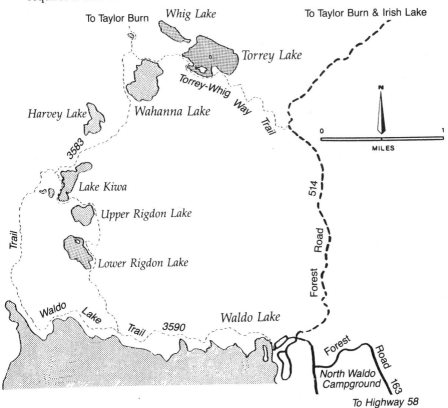

36
Trillium Lake

Clackamas County
Mt. Hood National Forest
Distance from Portland: 55 miles

Being at Trillium Lake feels like sitting inside a picture postcard, one that you might buy to send to friends in another part of the country just to show them that this kind of beauty really does exist. Its classic view of Mt. Hood shows up frequently in tourism books and brochures, and its easy accessibility from Portland makes it popular during the summer months. Although heavily fished, it can offer fair fly angling and some measure of seclusion in autumn.

Located on the south slope of Mt. Hood, the breezy lake often sports sailors (in small craft) and windsurfers. Swimming also fills a summer afternoon nicely, or you can just float in the sun and marvel at the beauty of Mt. Hood.

Originally a small, seven-acre lake, Trillium was expanded in 1960 to nearly 60 acres by the damming of Mud Creek. The lake's depth reaches only 16 feet at its deepest point near the dam, and more than three-fourths of the lake is shoal area, less than 10 feet deep.

Heavily fished, the lake sports stocked rainbow, primarily, and a few native brook and cutthroat trout. The rainbow average eight to nine inches, but have been caught above 14.

A well-developed campground for both tent and trailer campers lies on the east side, but few campsites sit right on the lake. The popular campgrounds fill to capacity by noon on Fridays in midsummer. Facilities include tables, fire places, cook stands, drinking water, garbage containers, and flushies to make it worth the fee charged. The Forest Service also maintains boat ramps and day-use picnic areas at the lake.

Trillium Lake lies about four miles from Government Camp, the nearest source of supplies. Turn south from U.S. Highway 26 directly across from the Snow Bunny Lodge turnoff and follow Forest Road 2656 two miles south to the lake.

Photograph courtesy of the Oregon Department of Tourism   Trillium Lake & Mt. Hood

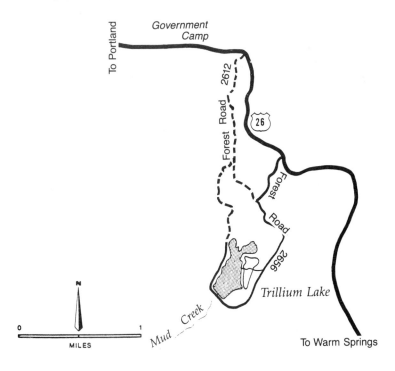

37
Twin Lakes

Deschutes County
Deschutes National Forest
Distance from Bend: 38 miles

These mountain lakes number among the most prominent type of lakes in Oregon, those filling craters left by volcanic activity. But the remarkable similarity of size and shape in North and South Twin Lakes make them geologically unique. They occupy maars, volcanic craters formed when hot magma pushed up into wet ground, creating an explosion of boiling steam that blasted large holes in the earth.

North Twin offers a more primitive experience, with a 20-site semi-improved campground on the north shore, which also provides a boat launch area. There's no drinking water at the lake, but no camping fee, either. This 112-acre lake receives only moderate use, compared with the popularity of South Twin. The ground has virtually been cleared of downed firewood, so you might want to bring your own. Or you can purchase firewood at the Twin Lakes Resort on South Twin.

The 100-acre southern lake is more popular, most likely because of the improvements—two large campgrounds with all the modern conveniences—and the small resort. The resort store has groceries and supplies for sale, row and paddle boats for rent, as well as a small restaurant and rustic cabins. You can rent time with a hot shower or do your laundry here for a fee.

Both lakes attract anglers, but the midsummer weekend activity on South Twin tends to make the fish a bit scarce. Stocked annually, the rainbow and kokanee in North Twin average eight to 10 inches. Popular methods include trolling with bait or lures or drifting with the wind and a fly.

Rainbow in South Twin stocked each spring sometimes grow to 15 inches. Still fishing with bobber and bait or slow trolling both yield results.

For another kind of fishing, just walk across the road about 200 yards to an arm of Wickiup Reservoir, which sports kokanaee, coho, German browns, and redsides (a type of rainbow trout named for their unusually bright side stripes). Motors are allowed on the reservoir.

Both North and South Twin provide good waters for swimming, and the 4,339-foot elevation is not too high for Central Oregon, where the sun seems to shine sooner, longer, and hotter.

These lakes are accessible in late April via Highway 97, or by June if you come by way of Century Drive; the Bend Ranger District can confirm. Century Drive (Cascade Lakes Highway 46) is longer but more scenic, passing several lakes along the way. It's about 65 miles along this route to Forest Road

South Twin Lake

42, which turns east 4½ miles to Forest Road 4260, leading to both lakes.

Or, you can take U.S. Highway 97 south from Bend about 16 miles to Forest Road 42, which crosses the Deschutes River after about 6 miles. From this crossing, follow Road 42 another 16 miles to Forest Road 4260 and turn south to the lakes.

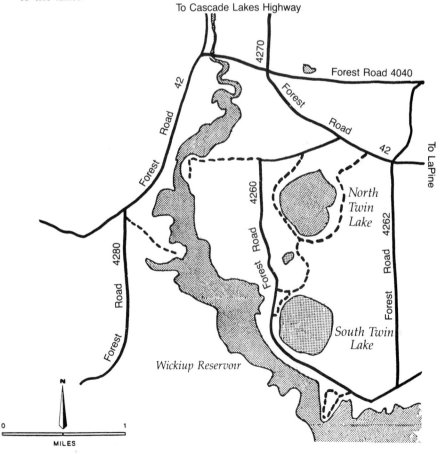

38

Upper Klamath Lake

Klamath County
Winema National Forest
Distance from Klamath Falls: 32 miles

Canoeing past red-winged blackbirds perched as sentinels atop tall bull-rushes, you watch a caspian tern shudder and plunge into the still water of Crystal Creek. Overhead, a pair of American white pelicans spiral in perfect formation on high zephyrs.

Meandering through the 15,000-acre freshwater marshes of the Upper Klamath National Wildlife Refuge, the six-mile Upper Klamath Canoe Trail begins in Pelican Bay, the northwest corner of this huge lake, and offers a great day of canoeing. Although motorboats are allowed, their speed is limited to 10 miles per hour. Few motorboats travel the waterways of the canoe trail, save those belonging to residents along Recreation Creek.

The wildlife refuge provides birdwatching at its best. Several species such as white pelicans, from which the bay takes its name, and bald eagles, seen only occasionally in other parts of the country, are abundant here. More than 250 species of birds frequent the marshes, including some 170 that nest here. Watch for tundra swans, avocets, black-crowned night herons, great egrets, marsh hawks, cinnamon teal, and wood ducks. (You can obtain a checklist and a map of the canoe trail from the Oregon Department of Fish and Wildlife in Klamath Falls.)

To complete the six-mile loop, plan for a full day of leisurely paddling. The closest launch site is at Rocky Point Public Boat Launch, about three miles northeast of Highway 140 off West Side Road. Maps of the trail are available at the launch site and at the Rocky Point Resort. Or you can stop by the Klamath Ranger District Headquarters at 1936 California Avenue in Klamath Falls.

From Rocky Point, canoe north into Recreation Creek. The route is signed, but only at somewhat lengthy intervals. After about 1½ miles, you'll head south on Crystal Creek, which takes you back into Pelican Bay.

For a shorter trip (3½ miles), after proceeding south on Crystal Creek, turn west and cut through a large open "lake" within the marsh (motors are prohibited here), back to Recreation Creek. Finding the signs in this area can sometimes be an adventure, but Mt. Harriman and Greylock Mountain to the south and Pelican Butte to the northwest provide ready landmarks.

You'll want to bring mosquito repellent along, and a hat and sunscreen provide good protection against the hot southern Oregon sun. Also, a day of paddling can be exhausting if you don't bring along some drinking water.

Pelican Bay offers good rainbow trout fishing, which is especially good off the fishbanks, the name locals give to the tip of marshland south from where Crystal Creek enters the bay. Most anglers here consider anything under four pounds not worth keeping.

Fishing licenses and tackle—and the latest scoop on where the trout are biting—are available at both Rocky Point and Harriman Springs resorts, where you can also rent canoes and boats with or without motors.

Harriman Springs Resort, on West Side Road two miles from Highway 140, provides a public launch. From here, canoeists can explore Harriman Creek and an open marsh area where beaver and muskrat are often seen, or paddle the two miles north to start the canoe trail.

You can easily spend several days wandering over the refuge area. Camping is free at two primitive campgrounds, Odessa to the south and Malone Springs to the north. Both have boat launch areas and are about four miles by water from the canoe trail.

The resorts house restaurants and lodging, and reservations for cabins are essential. Write to Rocky Point Resort, Harriman Rt. Box 92, Klamath Falls 97601; or to Harriman Springs Resort, Harriman Rt. Box 79, Klamath Falls 97601.

To get to the launch site at Rocky Point, take Highway 140 northwest from Klamath Falls about 27 miles to West Side Road, which turns right (northeast) about five miles to the boat launch. This area is generally accessible year-round, but the resorts often close for the winter.

Canoe Trail on Upper Klamath Lake

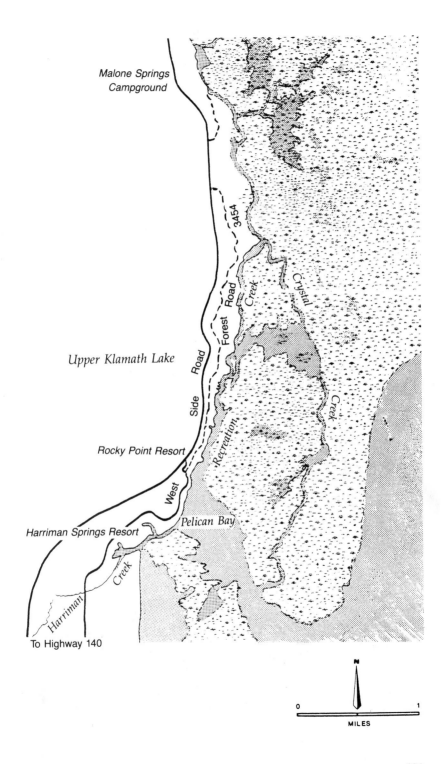

Malone Springs
Campground

3454

Forest Road

Crystal

Creek

Upper Klamath Lake

Road

Side

Creek

Rocky Point Resort

Recreation

West

Pelican Bay

Harriman Springs Resort

Creek

Harriman

To Highway 140

N

0   1

MILES

121

39
Wahtum Lake

Hood River County
Mt. Hood National Forest
Distance from Portland: 90 miles

Located in the newly designated Columbia Wilderness Area, Wahtum Lake is hidden deep within the folds of Mt. Hood's north slope. The steep foothills rising above Wahtum Lake give one the sense of being remote, isolated. A short, ¼-mile trail leads down to the 62-acre cirque, carved by glacial erosion. The lake reaches a maximum depth of 184 feet near the center and takes its indigo hue from its deep, clear waters.

The abundance of wild huckleberries and blueberries once drew Native American Indians to Wahtum Lake for an annual harvest. The name comes from the Sahaptin word for pond or body of water.

The Forest Service maintains a small camp area next to the road, and a few natural sites line the lake's southeastern shore. The fishing for brook and rainbow trout rates only fair here, with bait fishing the most popular. Fly angling can be productive in early morning and evening hours. You might also want to throw a line in at Scout Lake, a small brook trout lake just south of Wahtum on the same road.

Hiking opportunities abound, with the Pacific Crest National Scenic Trail bordering the north, east, and south sides of the lake. If you can arrange a drop-off and pick-up, you'll find the 14-mile hike from Wahtum along Trails 435 and 440 down to the Columbia Gorge incredible. The trail follows Eagle Creek as it tumbles over a series of waterfalls along the way. A one-way trip along this trail is definitely easiest starting at Wahtum rather than the other way around—the last half of the trail going in to Wahtum climbs nearly 3,500 feet.

Wahtum Lake is located about 13 miles by road north of the more popular Lost Lake (see separate entry). To get there, take State Highway 35 south from Hood River, following signs to Dee, the nearest source of supplies. From there, follow Forest Road 13 toward Lost Lake, taking the north (right) fork after about three miles. Drive another four miles to Forest Road 1310 and turn right (north) about six miles to Wahtum. Road 13 is paved, and 1310 is generally in very good condition, although it may occasionally be obstructed by logging operations in the area. In general, you can get into Wahtum Lake shortly after the first of June.

Wahtum Lake at dusk

Trail

Creek

Eagle

To Eagle Creek Park

Trail

440

Pacific

Crest

Wahtum Lake

Forest Road 1310

Scout Lake

To Forest Road 13

N

0   1

MILES

40
Walton Lake

Crook County
Ochoco National Forest
Distance from Bend: 68 miles

Met at the shoreline by stands of timber on three sides and a meadow on the fourth, Walton looks more like a natural lake than a reservoir, but it was first created in the 1900's with the damming of Camp Creek. At 18 acres, Walton's size also contrasts with the typical image of a reservoir.

Originally called Kings Reservoir, the lake provided a water source for early gold mining. In the 1960's, in cooperation with the Forest Service, the Izaak Walton League constructed the dam that exists today and renamed the lake in honor of their well-known patron.

Predictably, fishing attracts the greater number of visitors once the lake becomes accessible, usually early in May. The Oregon Department of Fish and Wildlife stocks the lake regularly with legal-sized rainbow.

The Forest Service charges a nightly fee for staying in the campground. Located on the north and south shores, the campground has several nice sites that sit right on the lake, and it fills nearly every summer weekend. Both spring and well water run cold from tap or pump for drinking, and site facilities include tables and fire places. Some folks enjoy swimming in Walton Lake from June or July on. The lake reaches a depth of only 21 feet at its deepest, and the sun in this part of Oregon shines particularly hot.

Hikers might want to take a day to head up Round Mountain. The trail starts at Walton Lake and climbs some six miles to the top, where the view stretches across the forests to Three Sisters in the west and Mt. Hood to the north.

To reach Walton Lake, which lies about 30 miles northeast of Prineville, take U.S. Highway 26 east about 16 miles to County Road 123. Proceed nine miles to the Ranger Station, then turn left on Forest Road 22, which follows Ochoco Creek northeast another seven miles to the campground. The road is paved all the way in, and a paved campground road circles the lake. A boat ramp sits on the west shore.

Photograph courtesy of the U.S. Forest Service

Walton Lake

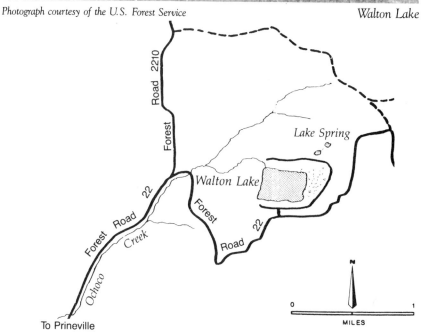

Appendix

Lake Name	U.S.G.S. Topographic Quadrangle
1 Anthony Lakes	Anthony Lakes Quadrangle
2 Betty Lake	Waldo Lake Quadrangle
3 Blow & Doris Lakes	Elk Lake Quadrangle
4 Bobby Lake	The Twins Quadrangle
5 Breitenbush Lake	Breitenbush Hot Springs Quadrangle
6 Campbell & Dead Horse Lakes	Lee Thomas Quadrangle
7 Charlton Lake	The Twins Quadrangle
8 Clear Lake	Three Fingered Jack Quadrangle
9 Cottonwood Meadow Lake	Cougar Peak Quadrangle
10 Daly & Parrish Lakes	Coffin Mountain Quadrangle
11 Devils Lake	Three Sisters Quadrangle
12 Frog Lake	Wapinitia Pass Quadrangle
13 Gold Lake	Waldo Lake Quadrangle
14 Hemlock Lake	Quartz Mountain Quadrangle
15 Hideaway Lake	Mt. Mitchell Quadrangle
16 Hosmer Lake	Elk Lake Quadrangle
17 Irish & Taylor Lakes	Irish Mountain Quadrangle
18 Link Creek Basin Lakes	Three Fingered Jack Quadrangle
19 Linton Lake	Three Sisters Quadrangle
20 Lost Lake	Bull Run Lake Quadrangle
21 Lucky Lake	Elk Lake Quadrangle
22 Marion Lake	Mt. Jefferson Quadrangle
23 Olallie Lake	Breitenbush Hot Springs Quadrangle
24 Opal & Timpanogas Lakes	Cowhorn Mountain Quadrangle
25 Pamelia Lake	Mt. Jefferson Quadrangle
26 Roslyn Lake	Bull Run Quadrangle
27 Round Lake	Three Fingered Jack Quadrangle
28 Scott Lake	Three Sisters Quadrangle
29 Sparks Lake	Broken Top Quadrangle
30 Square Lake	Three Fingered Jack Quadrangle
31 Squaw Lakes	Squaw Lakes Quadrangle
32 Summit Lake	Timothy Lake Quadrangle
33 Three Creeks Lake	Broken Top Quadrangle
34 Todd Lake	Broken Top Quadrangle
35 Torrey Lake	Waldo Mountain Quadrangle
36 Trillium Lake	Mt. Hood South Quadrangle
37 Twin Lakes	Davis Mountain Quadrangle
38 Upper Klamath Lake	Pelican Bay Quadrangle
39 Wahtum Lake	Wahtum Lake Quadrangle
40 Walton Lake	Lookout Mountain Quadrangle*

*Walton Lake was created in the 1960s and does not appear on the 15-minute topographic map made in 1951. The U.S.G.S. is in the process of converting all 15-minute maps to 7½-minute scale, which should be completed by 1990. Walton Lake will appear on the larger-scale map.

Index

The text of this book
was composed in Goudy Old Style.
Typeset by Corvallis Typesetting,
Corvallis, Oregon.